1997

Building the Foundations of Faith

The Religious Knowledge, Beliefs, and
Practices of Catholic Elementary School
Teachers of Religion

Rev. Paul W. Galetto, OSA, Ph.D.
Villanova University

Department of Elementary Schools
National Catholic Educational Association

Dedication

I dedicate this work to all the teachers in the front lines of Catholic education and the great sacrifices they make for the faith of the Church. I most especially remember my late sister, Sr. Marie Pierre, DM, who was a great teacher, administrator, and religious. Her memory and example are alive today in the many people she taught.

I also dedicate this book to the many students in Catholic schools across our nation. May they benefit from the research as I have benefited from having taught them, most especially Thomas R. Fabietti (1967-1994).

Contents

Acknowledgments

I would like to thank all the thousands of teachers who took the time to provide the information that is used in this book. I greatly appreciate the contribution they make on a daily basis.

I owe a debt of gratitude to my brothers in the Augustinian Order for their encouragement and support in bringing this research to fruition. I also thank my family and friends for all the behind-the-scenes labor that went into this project.

Special thanks to Dr. John Convey of the Catholic University of America in Washington, D.C. His guidance, encouragement, and example have been instrumental causes in the realization of this work.

I would also like to thank Dr. Robert J. Kealey of the National Catholic Educational Association for his support in helping to bring this book to light.

For we are God's servants,
working together;
you are God's field, God's building.
According to the grace of God
given to me,
like a skilled master builder
I build the foundations of faith
and others build on what I have laid.

— 1 Corinthians 3:9-10

List of Tables

Preface

The Catholic elementary school teacher assists the Church in its evangelizing mission. Teachers do this by their instruction and example. This research report presents data about those Catholic elementary school teachers who daily teach and model religion to the students; they are the school's catechists. Two generations ago such a report would have been considered superfluous. During the past 50 years, however, a gradual transition has taken place among these catechists, from their being predominantly priests or members of religious communities to their being today almost exclusively laywomen and laymen. Because these catechists bear such a grave responsibility, those in leadership positions in the Catholic Church need to understand the background of these catechists, their understanding of the Catholic religion, their practice of their religion. In addition, these leaders need to know what factors have contributed to the positive formation of these catechists.

This research report presents the answers to these questions. Augustinian Father Paul W. Galetto conducted this research as part of his doctoral studies at The Catholic University of America. The National Catholic Educational Association was delighted that he selected this topic for his dissertation and assisted him with the research because hard data in these areas were seriously lacking. Father Galetto has not only analyzed the data but in his final chapter he offers some very thought-provoking suggestions for providing effective continuing education for these catechists.

The NCEA Department of Elementary Schools expresses its gratitude to Father Galetto for undertaking this research, for providing a readable analysis, and for offering meaningful suggestions. The accompanying pictures were all taken by him and remind the reader of those to whom the work of the catechists is directed. The department also expresses its gratitude to Tara McCallum, its editorial assistant, for her work on the manuscript and to Beatrice Ruiz, of the communications department of NCEA, who laid out the book.

The NCEA Department of Elementary Schools presents this work as the eighth part in its continuing research on Catholic elementary schools with the hope that all leaders in Catholic education will examine its contents thoughtfully and initiate ways to help our catechists as the Catholic Church moves into the second millennium.

Kieran Hartigan, RSM, P.D.　　　　　　　　　　　　　*Robert J. Kealey, Ed.D.*
President　　　　　　　　　　　　　　　　　　　　*Executive Director*

Feast of Pentecost 1996
NCEA Department of Elementary Schools

CHAPTER ONE

The Theory

Overview

Definitions of catechists, religion teachers, and Catholic school teachers abound (Buetow, 1988). In many areas these definitions are overlapping. Some focus more on who the particular teacher should be, some on what he or she should do. An understanding of the teacher of religion that helps to focus the perspective taken in the present work is one offered from the research done in religiosity, most especially the work of Stark and Glock (1968). They defined religiosity as having five major components: knowledge, belief, practice, experience, and consequence. These elements—with the exception of experience, which does not lend itself to the type of measurement used here—will serve to focus this study of Catholic school teachers of religion. Each of the four measurable components has a parallel in the current literature of the Catholic Church: knowledge of Church teaching (knowledge), fidelity to the Magisterium (belief), model of the Christian lifestyle (practice), and desire to see the faith engendered in the life of students (consequence). These characteristics go beyond pedagogical competence, something all teachers should possess, and they also apply to all teachers in a Catholic school. For the teacher of religion, however, they are of primary importance because they particularly define that role the teacher seeks to fill.

From its incipient days, Christianity has addressed the questions regarding the nature of the teacher of religion. Jesus was himself called "teacher" on many occasions. Even today He serves as the model for all teachers. In the patristic period of the Church, many authors wrote about the teacher and his or her call to serve the People of God. One of the finest descriptions of a teacher from this period comes from St. Augustine of Hippo (1978), who, in his work *The First Catechetical Instruction (De Catechizandis Rudibus)*, reflected on his own teaching experiences and offered suggestions for others who hoped to follow him:

> Let us adapt ourselves to our pupils with a love which is at once the love
> of a brother, of a father, and of a mother. When once we are linked to
> our students in heart, the old familiar things will seem new to us. So great

is the influence of a sympathetic mind, that, when our students are affected by us as we speak and we by them as they learn, we dwell in each other and thus they speak within us what they hear, while we learn in them what we teach. (XII, 17)

Indeed, in the history of the Church, everyone from philosophers to popes has written about the nature and qualities of teachers. To narrow the focus to the subject at hand, a delimitation of this study will be descriptors of religion teachers that have been written since the Second Vatican Council by authorities of the hierarchical church (i.e., popes, congregations, the National Conference of Catholic Bishops, and individual bishops).

Review of Catholic Church Literature

In examining the current literature of the Catholic Church regarding catechists, one finds an obvious lacuna is present. Although much of the literature focuses on the catechetical programs and the catechized, catechists themselves are not written about extensively in many of the most important documents. When the questions "What is a catechist?" and "How does one measure whether someone is an effective or affective catechist?" are asked, the hunt for descriptors yields a broad, confused, and inconsistent list of terms.

The current field of catechetics is relatively new, since its rebirth after the Second Vatican Council. The tone of the documents immediately following the council implied that members of religious congregations would be the catechists; the shift to lay involvement was not foreseen. Now that the Church is addressing the increased role of the laity in catechesis, the field is evolving. In several instances, the clearest statements of what a catechist should be seem to have been developed from moments of conflict in particular dioceses. Individual American bishops have entered the discussion and have established guidelines that begin to define a catechist. In the following, an attempt is made to cull from current Church literature a quantifiable definition of a catechist.

Knowledge of Church Teachings

In the Second Vatican Council's (1965a) "Declaration on Christian Education," it stated that teachers "should...be prepared for their work with special care, having the appropriate qualifications and adequate learning both religious and secular" (no. 8). This statement recognized that catechists must be sufficiently prepared to meet the demands placed upon them as teachers and people of faith.

The Congregation for the Clergy (1971), in the *General Catechetical Directory*, observed, "That a strong doctrinal heritage must be acquired is self-evident. This must always include adequate knowledge of Catholic doctrine together with a degree of scientific theology obtained at higher catechetical institutes. Sacred Scripture should be as it were the soul of the entire formation" (no. 112). This document takes for granted that the catechist is a priest or a religious.

The American hierarchy addressed this issue of knowledge of Church teachings in several places. In a paper entitled *A Report on the State of Catechesis in the United States*, the United States Catholic Conference (1990b) stated, "From their [the bishops'] comments it is clear that catechist formation is a high priority for many bishops, and that they are concerned about the quality of catechists in their diocese" (p. 33). It has become increasingly apparent that to be a qualified catechist, one must have an adequate knowledge of Church teachings. The United States Catholic Conference (1976, 1979, 1994b) has also issued three policy statements that address this particular concern: *Teach Them*, *Sharing the Light of Faith*, and "A Vision Statement for Catechesis."

Teach Them, a 1976 statement by the bishops on the importance of Catholic schools, specified that all who are in the school are responsible for its religious atmosphere. The document suggested that "doctrine" be a part of the educational approaches used to initiate new teachers in the schools. When teachers are aware of the faith and its importance in their own lives, they will carry out "the commitment of handing on the faith to the next generation, not merely preserved, but more glorious, more efficacious, more valued by those who in their turn will take up the charge to 'go and teach'" (no. 5).

The United States Catholic Conference issued *Sharing the Light of Faith* in 1979 as the application of the *General Catechetical Directory* to the local Church in the United States. Chapter 9 of the text was dedicated solely to catechists and most especially to their qualities, roles, and preparation. When addressing the desirable characteristics of the catechist, *Sharing the Light of Faith* stated:

> As important as it is that a catechist have a clear understanding of the teaching of the Christ and His Church, this is not enough. He or she must also receive and respond to a ministerial call, which comes from the Lord and is articulated in the local Church by the bishop. (no. 213)

With respect to the formation process of the catechist, *Sharing the Light of Faith* noted several times that knowledge of religious teaching is essential. It called for "instruction in theology and scripture" and "continuing in-service educational opportunities" (no. 213). Throughout the document, passing references were made to the cognitive aspects of religious education.

In the draft of a 1994 document that was to be issued with the publication of the *Catechism of the Catholic Church* in English, "A Vision

Statement for Catechesis," the bishops stated that the faith of the catechist must be both "well-informed and well-formed" (p. 8). They went on to say:

> Faith is well-informed by the authoritative Church teaching. . . . Christians should not be ignorant of any of the great truths of their faith, of the mystery of the Triune of God; of creation, of sin and the redemptive grace of Christ; of the unfolding action of the Spirit in the Church and in history, as well as in the moral life. (p. 8)

With this document and the publication of the *Catechism of the Catholic Church* itself, it seems evident that the Church has clarified successively its position that people teaching the faith need to be well-informed.

On the level of the local Church, this discussion about the catechist's knowledge of Church teachings has been the central focus of several writings. In 1974, Joseph L. Bernardin, as archbishop of Cincinnati, gave a talk addressing the roles of bishops, theologians, and religion teachers. Delineating the differences and obligations of each of these vocations, Bernardin said, "teachers of religion must at least provide [the student] with a clear and articulated presentation of what it is that the Church teaches" (p. 103). The obvious implication here is that the teachers cannot make such a presentation unless they have mastered the information themselves.

In 1977, while auxiliary bishop of Cincinnati, Daniel Pilarczyk presented a talk to the Catholic school principals and religion department heads. The talk, entitled "When Disputes Arise," addressed the rights and responsibilities of teachers and parents concerning religious matters. According to Pilarczyk, one of the teacher's primary responsibilities is that he or she "has to know what the church teaches and must present it in the most effective way possible, the way most likely to evoke acceptance and assent" (p. 265). To do otherwise, the bishop attested, "is equivalent to sending the bus driver into the kitchen to prepare the school lunch" (p. 265).

More recently, Bishop John Myers (1993) of Peoria, to resolve a "general feeling of uncertainty among catechists and parents" (p. 593), issued a pastoral letter in his diocese entitled "To Reach Full Knowledge of the Truth." Repeatedly, the document stressed the importance of catechists having a correct understanding of the Church's teachings. Citing *Catechesi Tradendae* of John Paul II (1979, no. 61), Myers wrote:

> Catechists for their part, must have the wisdom to pick from the field of theological research those points that can provide light for their own reflection and their teaching, drawing, like the theologians, from the true sources, in the light of the Magisterium. (no. 17)

It seems clear from the position of the hierarchy of the Church that a requisite quality of catechists is that they be well-informed about the teachings of the Church if they are to be qualified teachers of religion.

Fidelity to the Magisterium

The essence of good catechists is that they concentrate their teaching on what is found in the Magisterium of the Church.

In a talk that Pope John Paul II (1992) gave to the American bishops on the topic of Catholic elementary schools in the United States and the lay teachers in them, he said, "In regard to the content of religion courses, the essential criterion is fidelity to the teaching of the Church" (p. 179).

In an earlier document of the Congregation for Catholic Education (1982), *Lay Teachers: Witnesses to Faith*, this same issue was addressed. In talking about the school community, of which the teacher is of course a part, the document stated that being a member of the community "involves a sincere adherence to the Magisterium of the Church [which offers] a presentation of Christ as the supreme model of the human person" (no. 38).

Bernardin (1974) stressed the importance of catechists as being the "faithful collaborators of the bishops. They [catechists] must present the Church's teaching, and they must present it as the Church's teaching" (p. 102). Pilarczyk (1977) likewise stressed this point when he said, "First of all, teachers have the responsibility to teach full and unadulterated Catholic doctrine. This responsibility arises out of the demands of fidelity toward the church under whose aegis they work" (p. 265).

Documents published by the United States Catholic Conference have also addressed this issue. The clearest statements by the conference were found in *Sharing the Light of Faith* (1979) and *Guidelines for Doctrinally Sound Catechetical Materials* (1990a). In *Sharing the Light of Faith*, it stated that one of the primary characteristics of the catechist is exhibiting commitment to the Church:

> One who exercises the ministry of the word represents the Church, to which the word has been entrusted. The catechist believes in the Church. . . . The catechist realizes that it is the Christ's message which he or she is called to proclaim. To insure fidelity to that message, catechists test and validate their understanding and insights in the light of the gospel message as presented by the teaching authority of the Church. (no. 208)

In reference to the message that catechetical materials should have, the United States Catholic Conference (1990a), in *Guidelines for Doctrinally Sound Catechetical Materials*, stated:

The first principal of doctrinal soundness is that the Christian message be both authentic and complete. For expressions of faith and moral teachings to be authentic they must be in harmony with the doctrines and traditions of the Catholic Church, which are safeguarded by the bishops, who teach with unique authority. (p. 432)

Model of the Christian Lifestyle

If there is one theme that is repeated throughout the pertinent litera-ture, it is that the catechist, as well as all teachers in Catholic schools, should be a model of the Christian lifestyle. In no place was this better stated than in *Lay Teachers: Witnesses to Faith* by the Congregation for Catholic Educa-tion (1982):

The more completely an educator can give concrete witness to the model of the ideal person that is being presented to the students, the more this ideal will be believed and imitated for it will then be seen as something reasonable and worthy of being lived, something concrete and realizable. (no. 32)

Another document by the Congregation for Catholic Education (1988), *The Religious Dimension of Education in a Catholic School*, refers to the teachers' primary responsibility as the establishment of a religious dimension in the school: "Through this daily witness [of the teachers], the students will come to appreciate the uniqueness of the environment to which their youth has been entrusted. If it is not present, then there is little left which can make the school Catholic" (no. 26).

The Second Vatican Council's (1965a) "Declaration on Christian Education" called teachers to "bear testimony by their lives" (no. 8). They are to be examples for the students they teach. Cardinal Baum (1989), when addressing the American bishops at a meeting at the Vatican, reminded the bishops that they must provide lay teachers with the "formation they need in order to be the models and the source of the religious formation of our young people" (p. 709).

In *Sharing the Light of Faith*, the United States Catholic Conference (1979) emphasized the importance of teachers being a model of living the Christian life:

Teachers in Catholic schools are expected to accept and live the Christian message and to strive to instill a Christian spirit in their students. . . . The school's principal and faculty are responsible for making clear the impor-tance of religion. The quality of the catechetical experience in the school and the importance attached to religious instruction, including the amount of time spent on it, can influence students to perceive religion as either highly important or of little importance. (no. 232)

Desire to See the Faith Engendered in the Students' Lives

Concrete references to this characteristic of the catechist are found in three major sources: "Declaration on Christian Education" by the Second Vatican Council (1965a), *Sharing the Light of Faith* of the United States Catholic Conference (1979), and Bernardin's 1974 talk on religious education.

In the "Declaration on Christian Education," the Second Vatican Council placed great emphasis on the concept of education in general and then, more particularly, on the Catholic school. In discussing the Catholic school, it made references to teachers and their role in forming students in the faith:

> [Teachers] should strive to awaken in their pupils a spirit of personal initiative and, even after they have left school, they should continue to help them with their advice and friendship and by the organization of special groups imbued with the true spirit of the Church. The sacred Synod declares that the services of such teachers constitute an active apostolate, one which is admirably suited to our times and indeed is very necessary. (no. 8)

The council understood schools and teaching as agents of formation and change in the lives of the students, most especially spiritual change, so that there would be a preparation for the reality of the Kingdom of God. If a teacher were to be defined in terms of one task only, it would be as sculptor of the spiritual life of his or her students.

Sharing the Light of Faith had much more to say on this issue. In Chapter 9, "Catechetical Personnel," the document listed several desirable characteristics of the catechist. Four of them dealt directly with engendering the faith in the lives of the students:

1. Catechists are called to be "witnesses to the Gospel":

> To give witness to the Gospel, the catechist must establish a living, ever-deepening relationship with the Lord. He or she must be a person of prayer, one who frequently reflects on the scriptures and whose Christlike living testifies to deep faith. Only men and women of faith can *share faith with others*, preparing the setting within which people can respond in faith to God's grace [italics added]. (no. 207)

To be a witness and a catechist means to become actively engaged with others in their spiritual quest.

2.   Catechists are called to exhibit "commitment to the Church": "Committed to the visible community, the catechist strives to be an instrument of the Lord's power and a sign of the Spirit's presence" (no. 208). Commitment implies action. The catechist is called to do more, to be more, and to be an instrument of service.

3.   Catechists are called to be "sharers in the community." The catechist learns the value of the community by experiencing it (no. 209). It is in being active that the catechist fulfills his or her role.

4.   Catechists are called to be "servants of the community":

> Authentic experience of Christian community leads one to the service of others. The catechist is committed to serving the Christian community, particularly in the parish, and the community at-large. Such service means not only responding to needs when asked, but taking the initiative in seeking out the needs of individuals and communities and *encouraging students to do the same* [italics added]. (no. 210)

This is the clearest endorsement of this dimension. It is not enough simply to be involved in the life of the parish (i.e., to be a model of the Christian lifestyle), but the catechist must encourage others to do the same. The catechist is the instrument by which the community seed is watered and nourished. It is not enough just to have seeds; they must be encouraged to bud and blossom.

Bernardin (1974), in the talk cited earlier, when he was describing the qualities of the teacher of religion, wrote:

> Obviously [teachers of religion] must be concerned about personal growth in faith on the part of their students. This is what Christian education is all about. Sometimes, to the great sorrow of the teacher of religion, this personal growth does not take place. (p. 103)

For Bernardin, the teacher's desire to see the faith engendered in the life of the student is more than merely a "concern"; it must be an active ministry. He went on to say that the best way to do this is through a faithful presentation of the Church's teachings.

Fr. Edward Braxton (1986) explained the nature of this dimension of engendering faith in the lives of students. He cited the role of the catechist as one who "forms, informs and transforms in Christ" (p. 491). In addressing catechists directly, he wrote, "If you are to help them [students] to experience faith and to know the implications of that faith in their daily lives, they must actually participate in your living faith" (p. 491).

For Braxton, education is far more than an ideology; it is a radical discovery of the self before God. Thus, the teacher, with the students, must become actively engaged in this quest. The teacher and students must be spiritual companions. The catechist must not simply exhort the students to pray, but he or she must pray with them and let them learn from the catechist how to pray. In concluding his talk, Braxton offered St. Augustine as the model for all catechists. Recalling Augustine's monumental tome, *The City of God*, Braxton noted:

> For the catechist this is a very strong reminder that the young disciples in his [or her] care have a mission; they must be directed to an active lay apostolate even as children and teenagers. As adults they must bring their Christian vision to the shaping of history around them. (p. 496)

Indeed, for catechists, knowledge, belief, and modeling the Christian lifestyle are not enough. Catechists are not satisfied until they have helped others to share fully their faith with them.

Summary

Among the many objectives that a teacher of religion must master, several come to the fore: having knowledge of Church teachings, personally believing those teachings, offering one's life as a model of the Christian lifestyle, and desiring to engender faith in the lives of one's students. Each of these complements the many other qualities that the good teacher of religion (or for that matter, any teacher) must possess: pedagogical competence, compassion, communication skills, etc.

As was noted earlier, depending on the perspective of the observer, a host of descriptors exists that define the teacher of religion. For some people the four qualities that serve as the focus of this book will not be listed among their top choices when selecting a teacher of religion; however, it cannot be denied that these qualities must figure in the mix of the ingredients in the recipe for success.

CHAPTER TWO

Survey and Data

Survey Composition and Distribution

During the 1993-1994 academic year, there were 7,114 Catholic elementary schools in the United States (Brigham, 1994). Virtually all of these schools were members of the National Catholic Educational Association (NCEA). There was a total of 112,199 teachers in Catholic elementary schools, 89.5% of whom were lay teachers. This total was the population used for this study and analyzed by use of cluster sampling. (It must be noted that not all teachers in Catholic elementary schools teach religion, but those teachers who do not are the exceptions.)

A systematic cluster sample of 10% (714) of the schools was taken from this population. The random selection of the sample was computer-generated through the offices of NCEA, choosing every 10th school, listed in zip-code order. Every state except Utah and Alaska was included, as well as the Bahamas, the Virgin Islands, and Puerto Rico.

An advance letter addressed to the school principal, mailed February 28, 1994, solicited volunteers to participate in the survey and asked the number of possible respondents in the school. The number of respondents was determined by the number of teachers of religion. The survey was given to both lay and religious faculty members of every school. Of the 714 schools that received this letter, 442 volunteered to participate in the study.

The final mailing of the surveys to the 442 schools was on April 12, 1994. Each survey packet included a cover letter explaining the purpose of the survey, the number of questionnaires appropriate for the school (as was indicated on a pre-response card that was mailed on February 28, 1994), and individual prestamped, preaddressed return envelopes for each questionnaire. A total of 4,375 surveys were mailed. Although the survey was anonymous, individual questionnaires were numbered for control purposes and for following up teachers who had not responded to the initial mailing. Confidentiality was preserved by using individual response envelopes.

The respondents were given several weeks to complete the survey.

They returned their surveys to the researcher in a preaddressed return envelope, which helped to prevent anyone from examining the responses and to minimize the risk of teachers giving socially desirable responses. Follow-up phone calls were made to those schools that had not responded by May 11, 1994.

Of the 4,375 surveys mailed to teachers in the 442 schools, 2,676 were returned from 419 schools; 98 (.04%) of these returns were discarded because they were improperly completed. Of the 2,578 valid surveys that were used for this study, 287 were from members of religious congregations and 2,291 were from the lay teachers of religion. The valid response rate was 58.9% for the respondents and 94.8% for the schools that agreed to participate in the survey.

The survey was presented in a machine-readable format to facilitate the collation of results. Received surveys were cataloged and entered into the computer database.

The questionnaire in this study, which had 128 items in four sections, included dichotomous and nondichotomous items, multiple-choice answers, Likert scales, and options for written responses. The estimated completion time was 20 to 25 minutes, although some respondents reported spending about 1 hour.

The survey instrument (see the Appendix) had several distinct parts. Section I, General Information, was subdivided into three parts. Part A (12 questions) dealt with personal background information that requested the gender, race, age, religious status, education, and marital status of the individual. Part B (11 questions) dealt with the particular teaching situation of the respondent, including locality of the school, percentage of Catholic students, years of teaching, religious education certification status, and description of the students. Part C (29 questions) requested information about teacher sentiment. The first 12 questions dealt with teacher opinion. These were questions about the teachers' sense of enjoyment and accomplishment as well as the achievement of their students. A set of six questions dealt with the teacher's sense of efficacy, distinguishing between religion-teaching efficacy and overall-teaching efficacy. In addition, three other subsets of questions attempted to ascertain general information about the teaching of religion (four questions), the religious environment of the school (five questions), and the teacher's perception of salary (two questions).

The questions for Section I were derived from three sources. First, general surveys given to teachers were examined and items were chosen that would prove beneficial for this study. Second, some questions were specifically designed for this study. Third, after a pilot study had been made, several issues arose that necessitated adding and deleting other questions.

Section II of the survey, Appraisal of Church Teaching, presented 25 issues, each followed by between three and five one-sentence statements that reflected varying positions on the particular issue. The respondent was asked to identify the statement that came closest to the Church's position on the particular issue and then to identify the statement that came closest to his or her own on that same issue (a total of 50 questions).

The issues represented four major areas: general Christian belief, Catholic dogma, Catholic moral teaching, and Catholic discipline. Issues were selected based on three perspectives. First, items were chosen based on three sources: similar studies that have been conducted of high school teachers, most notably Benson and Guerra's 1985 *Sharing the Faith: The Beliefs and Values of Catholic High School Teachers*; a listing of Catholic teachings found in the preliminary outline of the *Catechism of the Catholic Church* (United States Catholic Conference, 1994a); and suggestions by the International Council for Catechesis (1990) regarding the content of adult catechesis:

> Catechesis has to present in a comprehensive and systematic way the great *themes of the Christian religion* which involve faith and reasons for believing: the mystery of God and the Trinity, Christ, the Church, the sacraments, human life and ethical principles, eschatalogical realities, and other contemporary items in religion and morality. It will respect the hierarchy of truths and their interrelationship. (no. 43)

Second, issues were chosen because of their basic nature. Stark and Glock (1968), who completed a study of American religiosity, explained it best when they wrote:

> To most readers the questions we asked will seem extremely obvious and easy. Indeed, several theologians who assisted us in fashioning the questionnaire felt that to use these questions to measure religious knowledge and to speak of them as assessing the degree to which people have grasped the cultural heritage of their faith demeans that heritage. From the point of view of a sophisticated person we readily admit that the items used in this chapter touch only the most obvious portions of the Christian cultural heritage. (p. 141)

Third, issues were chosen that could be adapted to the response format.

After their original writing, the items were discussed and revised according to the comments of theologians and canon lawyers from several different parts of the country. Eight educators from across the nation who are affiliated with NCEA were also consulted, and further revisions were made based on their comments. The pilot study results dictated additions and deletions to correct errors that had been detected.

Section III of the survey dealt with religious practice, devotional and ritualistic. The 16 items were developed using Benson and Guerra's 1985 study and input from several other sources, mostly people familiar with Catholic devotion, ritual, and practice. Items were adjusted based on the comments of the national committee who reviewed the survey and on the written suggestions of the participants in the pilot study.

Section IV (10 questions) was derived from two sources. The first is Stark and Glock's (1968) description of the consequential dimension. What was being assessed here was the teacher's desire to see that the faith that he or she holds takes root in the lives of the students. This led to the second source for this survey, which is twofold: Thomas Groome's (1980) work *Christian Religious Education: Sharing Our Story and Vision* and a document by the United States Catholic Conference (1972), *To Teach as Jesus Did.* Both of these works describe three aspects of faith: affective, behavioral, and cognitive. Each aspect calls forth different responses from an individual: Affect calls forth trust; behavior, action; and cognition, knowledge. The purpose of this section was to ascertain the aspect from which a catechist primarily operates. The behavioral aspect calls forth a response to engage with others; affect and cognition are more private and personal in their orientation. The 10 questions in the survey were of two types: process and outcome. Processes are the methods or approaches that a teacher uses in the teaching of religion. Outcomes are the desired results that a teacher wishes to see in his or her students. A catechist who is high on the behavioral aspect in both subscales can be regarded as faithful to the consequential dimension in the model used in this study.

Analysis of the Data

Descriptive statistics, *t* tests, cross tabulations, regression analysis, and ANOVA were performed with the Statistical Package for the Social Sciences (SPSS) computer software. The first level of analysis was the compilation of frequencies for the different levels within each variable. Cross tabulations were done on the relevant personal background variables in order to discover any significant relationships. After a visual and logical analysis based upon a review of the literature and the information available, specific variables were selected for their entry into a regression analysis. These variables were cross-referenced using the Pearson Correlation Coefficients to determine the degree of multicollinearity, a statistical occurrence that, when high, comprises the determination of the relative importance of the predictors in the regression.

The dependent measures were tabulated before any regression analysis was undertaken. The first of these was a score for knowledge of Church teachings. The Appraisal of Church Teachings section asked teachers to examine 25 issues. With each issue were three, four, or five statements that reflected various theological perspectives on the issue. Teachers were asked to choose the statements that came closest to reflecting the Church's position on the issue. Dichotomous scoring was used: If teachers chose the statement that came closest to the Church's position, they received a score of 1; if not, they received a 0. The highest possible score was 25.

The same series of issues was used to determine a personal-belief score, which was the second dependent measure. Teachers were asked to choose which among the three, four, or five statements came closest to their personal position on the issue. Again, using dichotomous scoring, if they chose the statement that came closest to the Church's position, they received a 1; if not, a 0.

The third dependent measure was an efficacy score. There were two efficacy scores: religion-teaching efficacy and overall-teaching efficacy. Of the six questions in the instrument dealing with efficacy, three related to teaching religion and three to overall teaching. The responses to the questions were on a four-step Likert scale that was labeled *Strongly agree* to *Strongly disagree*. When items were negatively worded, reverse scoring was used. If a teacher did not respond to any item, no score was tabulated for that particular issue. The highest possible score for each scale was 12.

The major sets of predictors were of three types: personal background variables, devotional and ritual variables, and teacher-opinion variables. The last set of variables was used only for the regression of the efficacy measures.

The data presented in this study represent the percentages of those teachers who responded to the valid surveys received. For some questions, there are missing data because not all teachers gave a response for that particular question.

CHAPTER THREE

Background Information on Teachers

Personal Backgrounds of Teachers

Table 1 displays the personal characteristics of all of the teachers in this study. The sample of lay teachers is 95% female, 94% white, and 96% Catholic (of whom 8% are converts to Catholicism). Sixty-nine percent of the lay teachers are married (without having been married previously), and 55% have children living at home. Slightly more than 90% do not feel that the demands made on them as a lay teacher of religion conflict with their home duties.

Nearly 40% of the teachers are over age 45. Those under age 45 more broadly reflect the influence of the Second Vatican Council on their personal formation.

Table 1: Personal Characteristics of Teachers		
	% Laity	**% Religious**
Gender		
Female	95.3	96.2
Male	4.6	3.8
Race		
American Indian/Alaskan	0.3	0.3
Asian/Pacific Islander	0.7	1.4
Black, non-Hispanic	2.1	0.3
Hispanic	2.7	2.4
White or other	94.1	95.1
Age		
Under 25	5.8	0.0
25-34	23.8	6.6
35-44	30.4	10.8
45-54	28.9	28.6
55 or older	11.0	54.0

(table continues)

	% Laity	% Religious
Faith		
Catholic	88.2	98.6
Convert	7.7	1.4
Non-Catholic	3.6	0.0
Marital/Vocational status		
Religious (sister or brother) or priest	0.0	100.0
Single	20.7	0.0
Married	69.0	0.0
Widowed	2.7	0.0
Separated/Divorced (but not remarried)	5.5	0.0
Remarried after a divorce and annulment	1.5	0.0
Remarried after a divorce without an annulment	0.7	0.0
Children living at home		
Yes	55.3	0.0
No	44.3	96.9
Teacher demands conflict with home responsibilities		
Strongly disagree	30.3	45.3
Disagree	61.2	51.2
Agree	5.8	1.7
Strongly agree	1.6	1.0
Salary		
More than adequate	0.4	5.2
Adequate	23.1	65.2
Inadequate	51.5	19.2
More than inadequate	24.3	2.4
Volunteer (no salary received)	0.5	4.9
Parish financial contribution pattern		
My teaching in a Catholic school does not affect the amount I contribute in my parish offering.	69.2	57.8
Since I teach in a Catholic school, I give less than I would otherwise in my parish offering.	22.9	4.9
Since I teach in a Catholic school, I do not feel I need to make an additional contribution through my parish offering.	7.5	19.9

Note: For this and other tables in this chapter, all percentages may not equal or total 100%, either because percentages were rounded off or because not every teacher responded to each question.

The cross tabulation of the lay teachers' religion by race reveals that within the black/non-Hispanic population, over 25% are converts and another 25% are non-Catholic. Hispanics are mostly (98%) Catholic. Slightly more than 7% of white/other teachers are converts and 3% are non-Catholic. (N.B.: The sample of American Indian/Alaskan teachers is too small to make any inferences.)

Age distribution for lay teachers among the races (on a percentage basis) is equal for blacks/non-Hispanics and whites/others (i.e., 60% are age 44 or younger and 40% are age 45 or older). Asians/Pacific Islanders are older as a group, with 60% being 45 or over. Hispanics are 3 times more likely to be under age 45 (75%) than age 45 or over (25%).

Even though over 75% of the lay teachers feel their salary is inadequate, nearly 70% state that this does not impact upon the amount of their parish contribution.

In general, the numbers given for the religious parallel the laity. Fewer religious teach blacks/non-Hispanics (0.3% versus 2.1% for lay teachers). Religious tend to be much older than their lay counterparts: Eighty-two percent are age 45 or older versus 40% for lay teachers. By an almost 3-to-1 margin, when compared to lay teachers, religious tend to feel that their salary is adequate. Many religious did not respond to the question on contribution pattern (#48). In written comments returned with the survey, many religious state that they do not give to the parish collection because as members of religious communities, they feel they give more than enough through their vocation to serve the Church.

Preparation to Teach Religion

Most lay teachers of religion in this study completed college and obtained additional graduate credits, but few of them have graduate credits in theology. Approximately 8% of these teachers have no formal religious education (school-based or parish-based) before the age of 23 (the age limit set by this survey). Table 2 notes more than 25% of these teachers never attended Catholic elementary school; however, over 57% attended Catholic elementary school for 7 to 9 years. Over 30% of the lay teachers never attended Catholic high school, but 49% spent 4 or more years there. Nearly 44% have no Catholic collegiate education, but almost 30% have 4 or more years in Catholic college.

Table 2: Educational and Religious Formation Backgrounds of Teachers

	% Laity	% Religious
Educational level		
High school	0.8	0.3
College	24.7	9.4
College with graduate credits	51.1	25.8
Master's degree	12.0	26.5
Master's with graduate credit	10.9	38.0
Doctorate	0.3	0.0
Graduate credits in theology		
None	76.1	22.6
1-12	17.6	31.4
13-24	3.1	12.2
More than 24	2.5	33.4
Years of formal religious education before age 23 (parish or school)		
None	7.8	0.7
1-4	8.1	3.5
5-8	12.1	8.0
9-12	33.6	13.2
More than 12	38.1	74.2
Years of formal education in Catholic elementary school		
None	25.6	7.3
1-3	5.2	4.9
4-6	7.6	5.6
7-9	57.7	77.7
Years of formal education in Catholic high school		
None	34.0	10.5
1	1.6	1.7
2	1.8	2.8
3	2.1	4.9
4 or more	49.0	70.4

(table continues)

	% **Laity**	% **Religious**
Years of formal education in Catholic college		
None	43.9	4.9
1	4.1	2.8
2	5.3	7.0
3	2.1	6.3
4 or more	29.5	71.1
Experience of religious formation		
No religious formation	91.2	0.3
Initial formation only	2.6	0.3
Simple profession/minor orders only	2.7	13.2
Solemn vows or ordained (deacon or priest)	2.7	84.7

Cross tabulations reveal that in each racial and educational group, at least 45% of lay teachers have a college degree and additional graduate credits. With the exception of Hispanics, over 20% of each racial group have at least completed a master's degree. In each racial group, 75% of the respondents have no graduate credits in theology.

Age compared with formal religious education among lay teachers indicates that at least 2 out of 5 respondents over age 44 have more than 12 years of formal religious education. Only about 33% of each of the other age groups have more than 12 years of formal religious education. Although nearly 79% of Catholic lay teachers of religion have more than 8 years of religious education, less than 18% of converts and non-Catholics have as many years. Less than 10% of the teachers have any experience in religious formation involving a religious congregation or a seminary. Of lay respondents, 3% either made solemn vows in the religious institute or were ordained a deacon or priest.

Religious are more likely than their lay counterparts to have graduate credits and to have a master's degree. Over 75% of the religious have some credits in theology and nearly 75% have 12 or more years of religious education before the age of 23. Over 70% of the religious attended Catholic schools through college.

Teaching Situation

Table 3 presents the teachers' description of the school context. Teachers appear to be evenly distributed across grade levels. In the vast majority of schools, the student population is at least 90% Catholic. Lay teachers identify over 60% of the students as middle class and report that over 80% of the students are white/other, while blacks/non-Hispanics and Hispanics each comprise about 5% of the student body. Nearly 50% of the lay teachers identify their schools as suburban.

Table 3: Current Teaching Situation of Teachers		
	% Laity	**% Religious**
Grade level teaching		
Across levels	4.6	17.8
Pre-K to K	11.4	4.9
1st to 3rd	36.6	30.7
4th to 6th	31.0	22.6
7th to 8th	16.0	23.0
Locality of the school		
Inner city	7.5	16.4
City	30.5	30.3
Suburban	46.6	33.1
Rural	14.9	18.5
Percentage of Catholic students		
90-100%	79.0	69.3
60-89%	12.5	18.5
50-59%	2.5	2.1
40-49%	1.7	3.8
30-39%	1.2	1.0
Less than 30%	2.7	4.2
Where the teacher teaches religion		
Catholic school only	85.9	64.8
Catholic school and parish religious education program	14.0	35.2
Years teaching in Catholic school		
0-5	34.7	5.2
6-10	24.4	3.1
11-15	17.5	4.9
16-20	11.3	4.2
Over 20	12.0	82.6

(table continues)

	% Laity	% Religious
Years teaching religion		
0-5	37.8	5.2
6-10	24.4	4.9
11-15	16.1	4.9
16-20	10.7	6.3
Over 20	10.8	78.7
Economic status of majority of the teacher's religion students		
Poor	2.1	5.9
Lower middle	13.3	18.1
Middle middle	61.2	58.5
Upper middle	21.2	14.6
Wealthy	0.8	1.4
Ethnicity of majority of the teacher's religion students		
American Indian/Alaskan	0.5	1.4
Asian/Pacific Islander	1.4	2.1
Black, non-Hispanic	5.0	6.3
Hispanic	4.6	8.4
White or other	82.1	73.5
No majority	3.5	5.2

In almost all cases, lay teachers have been teaching religion as long as they have been teaching in Catholic schools. Newer teachers (between 0 and 5 years) predominantly teach each racial minority group of students. Three out of 5 teachers who have mostly black/non-Hispanic students are newer teachers. For Hispanic students, nearly 50% have newer teachers but majority white/other students have only about 33% newer teachers. Nearly 19% of those who teach religion to blacks/non-Hispanics are non-Catholics. Certified and non-certified teachers are uniformly spread throughout the racial population of students.

Black/non-Hispanic students comprise the largest racial group in all Catholic schools reported as less than 50% Catholic. White/other and Hispanic students are rarely found in schools that are less than 90% Catholic (14.3% and 15.6%, respectively). Over 70% of black/non-Hispanic students are in schools that teachers describe either as poor or lower middle class; 65% of Hispanics are in schools specified to be lower middle or middle middle class.

Nearly 90% of white/other students are in schools designated as middle middle class to upper middle class.

There is a difference between how lay teachers describe the locality of their school and how the school locations are identified by NCEA. In describing their teaching situation, 7.5% of these teachers designate their school as inner city; 30.5%, as city; 46.6%, as suburban; and 14.9%, as rural. The percentages specified in an NCEA report by Brigham (1994) are 12.9%, 32.9%, 30.9%, and 23.3%, respectively. The numbers for the religious are 16.4%, 30.3%, 33.1%, and 18.5%, respectively.

Slightly less than 80% of lay teachers designate their religion classes as composed of over 90% Catholic students. According to Brigham (1994), 10.4% of Catholic elementary school students are non-Catholic.

In this section there are several notable differences between religious and lay teachers of religion. Religious are more likely to teach in a parish religious education program besides their school teaching assignment than are lay teachers. Over 80% of the religious have taught for more than 20 years in Catholic schools. Religious appear slightly more likely to teach in schools with economically poor students and are more likely to teach upper grade levels and across grade levels. These teachers are more likely also to be found in inner-city schools.

Teaching Religion

In this study, 45% of the lay teachers are certified to teach religion through a diocesan program, and approximately 10% are certified through courses they took in college. Over 20% of the sample are attending certification courses while teaching religion and another 20% are teaching religion without certification. Table 4 relates the professional religion-teaching preparation of the religion teachers.

Table 4: Certification, Preparation, and Contractual Mandates of Teachers

	% Laity	% Religious
Certification to teach religion		
Certified by the (arch)diocese	45.1	56.4
Certified through college courses taken	10.8	33.1
Teaching while attending certification courses	21.3	4.5
Teaching without having undergone a certification program	22.2	5.9

(table continues)

	% Laity	% Religious
Preparation for certification to teach religion		
Never taken any informal or formal courses	9.3	0.3
Majority of preparation was informal instruction (e.g., local in-service programs, watching videos)	32.0	5.6
Majority of preparation was formal non-college credit courses (e.g., program sponsored by the diocese)	40.4	23.3
Majority of preparation was formal college credit courses	18.1	70.7
Diocesan requirements for permanent certification to teach religion		
1-2 courses	4.6	3.1
3-4 courses	10.0	5.9
5-6 courses	12.0	15.7
More than 6 courses	25.7	33.4
None	2.4	4.9
Unsure	42.0	29.6
Hours of updating received during current year		
None	23.7	18.5
1-8	36.0	30.7
9-16	23.8	22.3
17-24	7.9	7.0
More than 24	6.3	18.8
Is teaching religion mandated by contract?		
Yes	96.5	89.3
No	3.5	10.5
Would you choose to teach religion even if not mandated?		
Yes	83.2	94.4
No	16.0	4.2

The survey reveals that there is a wide variety of certification process requirements within the United States. Over 25% of the respondents have six courses or less for certification and another 25% have more than six courses. Over 40% of the teachers are unsure or unaware of the requirements for certification. Teachers report in written comments that accompanied the survey that several dioceses have no permanent certification process; in these dioceses, teachers are expected to continually update themselves.

Preparation for certification for lay teachers was received mostly through non-college credit courses (e.g., programs sponsored by the diocese) for 40% and informal instruction (e.g., in-service programs, watching videos) for 32%. Eighteen percent attended formal college courses for their certification program.

About 24% of the lay teachers received no updating in teaching religion during the 1993-1994 academic year in which the survey was conducted. Thirty-six percent had one day's worth (1-8 hours) of religious updating.

Fifty-seven percent of the lay Catholic teachers and 57% of the converts but less than 25% of the non-Catholics received certification by the diocese or through college courses. Nearly 21% of Catholics, 24% of converts, and 63% of non-Catholics are neither certified nor attending certification courses while teaching religion. About 7 out of 10 (69%) of those teaching religion with no certification are under age 34. Well over 66% of those over age 44 are certified either by the diocese or through college courses they have taken.

Religious are 3 times more likely than lay teachers to be certified to teach religion through college courses, which explains why such a large percentage of religious have formal college credit courses as their method of preparation to teach religion.

Devotional and Ritual Practices

Over 60% of each faith group (i.e., Catholics, converts, and non-Catholics) of lay religion teachers attend worship services at least once a week. Slightly more than 30% of non-Catholics attend on a less-than-weekly basis. In the *1995 Supplement of Religion in America*, the Princeton Religion Research Center reported that on a national scale, 47% of Catholics and 45% of Protestants have attended church in the last 7 days. This compares favorably with the approximately 90% of Catholic and converted lay teachers who attend worship services on at least a weekly basis. Table 5 lists the devotional and ritual practices of the lay and religious teachers in this survey.

Table 5: Frequency of Devotional and Ritual Practices of Teachers

	% Laity	% Religious
Attend worship services		
Every day	1.9	68.9
Several times per week	30.8	24.7
Once a week	55.2	5.9
2-3 times per month	7.0	0.3
Once a month	2.3	0.0
Several times per year	2.1	0.0
About once a year	0.3	0.0
Never	0.1	0.0
Recite the rosary		
Every day	4.8	43.6
Several times per week	7.1	16.0
Once a week	5.8	7.7
2-3 times per month	6.4	7.0
Once a month	6.6	3.1
Several times per year	34.1	14.3
About once a year	19.4	4.2
Never	15.3	3.8
Participate in a novena		
Every day	1.2	3.8
Several times per week	0.6	1.7
Once a week	1.6	4.2
2-3 times per month	1.0	4.9
Once a month	1.7	5.6
Several times per year	9.4	30.7
About once a year	24.5	22.6
Never	56.7	21.3
Read the Bible		
Every day	8.2	53.0
Several times per week	20.4	33.1
Once a week	11.7	4.9
2-3 times per month	15.3	2.8
Once a month	8.5	0.3
Several times per year	22.3	2.8
About once a year	5.8	0.3
Never	6.3	2.8

(table continues)

	% Laity	% Religious
Do non-biblical spiritual reading		
Every day	7.1	34.1
Several times per week	13.5	43.2
Once a week	9.8	7.7
2-3 times per month	13.1	6.3
Once a month	8.1	2.8
Several times per year	20.5	1.7
About once a year	9.5	0.0
Never	15.1	0.3
Do personal prayer		
Every day	81.0	94.8
Several times per week	12.3	3.8
Once a week	2.7	0.3
2-3 times per month	1.0	0.0
Once a month	0.3	0.0
Several times per year	0.7	0.0
About once a year	0.0	0.0
Never	0.2	0.0
Do private meditation		
Every day	39.4	83.6
Several times per week	26.8	11.5
Once a week	10.5	1.0
2-3 times per month	6.6	0.3
Once a month	3.8	1.0
Several times per year	5.3	0.0
About once a year	1.0	0.3
Never	4.2	0.0
Go to confession (reconciliation)		
Every day	0.1	0.3
Several times per week	0.2	0.0
Once a week	0.4	1.4
2-3 times per month	1.4	11.1
Once a month	3.6	26.1
Several times per year	26.2	42.5
About once a year	41.6	16.0
Never	24.8	1.0

(table continues)

	% Laity	% Religious
Say grace before meals		
Every day	62.1	88.5
Several times per week	20.5	7.7
Once a week	2.0	0.7
2-3 times per month	2.5	0.0
Once a month	1.2	0.0
Several times per year	5.8	0.3
About once a year	0.9	0.0
Never	2.0	0.0
Discuss your religious beliefs with others		
Every day	14.9	24.4
Several times per week	25.2	35.2
Once a week	9.1	10.1
2-3 times per month	13.1	13.2
Once a month	8.6	3.1
Several times per year	20.2	10.8
About once a year	4.4	0.3
Never	3.4	0.3
Visit or phone a friend or neighbor in need		
Every day	4.9	8.0
Several times per week	17.8	26.1
Once a week	16.9	22.0
2-3 times per month	22.3	20.6
Once a month	10.7	7.0
Several times per year	22.6	13.6
About once a year	2.8	1.0
Never	0.9	1.0
Take part in parish adult education program (Bible study, etc.)		
Every day	0.3	1.0
Several times per week	0.4	1.0
Once a week	4.2	10.1
2-3 times per month	2.2	3.8
Once a month	3.1	4.9
Several times per year	17.4	26.5
About once a year	28.1	21.6
Never	43.6	30.0

(table continues)

	% Laity	% Religious
Receive Communion		
Every day	2.4	69.7
Several times per week	29.3	24.0
Once a week	51.6	5.2
2-3 times per month	7.6	0.3
Once a month	3.3	0.0
Several times per year	2.8	0.0
About once a year	0.6	0.0
Never	1.0	0.0
Make a personal retreat		
More than once a year	4.2	25.8
Yearly	25.6	71.4
Every several years	11.1	1.7
Rarely	35.0	0.7
Never	23.7	0.0
Participate in inter-faith service		
More than once a year	8.1	12.5
Yearly	10.9	22.3
Every several years	8.6	13.2
Rarely	41.8	43.2
Never	30.1	8.0
Participate in renewal experiences (Marriage Encounter, Cursillo, RENEW, etc.)		
More than once a year	2.7	11.5
Yearly	3.7	10.8
Every several years	11.0	18.8
Rarely	33.4	32.4
Never	48.8	26.1

All faith groups participate in personal prayer, grace before meals, and meditation on an equal basis. Communion, which is a common practice in many Protestant faiths as well as the Catholic religion, is received on a weekly basis by over 85% of Catholic teachers and 90% of converts. Approximately 60% of non-Catholic teachers receive Communion on a monthly basis, and over 25% receive Communion less than once a year. Non-Catholic teachers and converts (over 60%) are more prone to discuss their faith with others on a weekly basis than are Catholic teachers (under 50%).

Several of the devotions or rituals are performed less than weekly but more frequently than several times a year by most lay teachers. Although 20% of Catholic teachers recite the rosary on a weekly basis, 48% do so on a monthly basis; these figures are also true for converts. Not surprisingly, about 66% of non-Catholic teachers hardly ever say the rosary, which is a particularly Catholic devotion. Converts and non-Catholics are much more likely to read the Bible on a weekly basis (55% and 60%, respectively) than are Catholics (38%). Seven percent of Catholic teachers never read the Bible. Percentages for non-biblical spiritual reading and the phoning of friends in need are the same for all faith groups.

Regarding the least frequently practiced devotional and ritual activities of the teachers, almost 90% of the non-Catholics and nearly 75% of the Catholics and converts participate in novenas less than once a year. Going to confession, a Catholic sacrament, is never done by 90% of non-Catholics and 20% of Catholics and converts. Fifty percent of Catholics and converts go to confession about once a year. About 66% of all faith groups attend adult education classes about once a year or less.

Well over 25% of each faith group of lay teachers make a yearly retreat, and nearly another 25% never make a retreat. Converts (30%) are twice as likely as Catholics (15%) to attend interfaith services, and non-Catholics (45%) are 3 times as likely as Catholics to do so. Approximately 33% of Catholics never attend such services. Well over 70% of each group rarely, if ever, attend renewal experiences such as RENEW, Cursillo, or Marriage Encounter.

As might be expected, religious are more frequent participants in ritual and devotional activities. When it comes to discussing one's religious beliefs with others, visiting or phoning a friend in need, and taking part in adult education, the percentage differences between religious and lay are only slight.

Summary of Personal Backgrounds of Teachers

Based upon the results of this study, the typical lay teacher of religion is female, white, married, and over age 40. She is a college graduate with additional graduate credits; however, none of these credits are in theology. Generally, this teacher completed the first 12 years of her early education in Catholic schools, which means she probably had at least 12 years of formal religious education by high school graduation.

She is certified to teach religion by the diocese through formal non-college credit courses and most probably has taught less than 10 years in Catholic schools. She teaches religion to a class of students who are at least

90% Catholic and come from white, middle-class families. She usually teaches 1st through 6th grade in a suburban school and feels that her salary is inadequate. This teacher attends Eucharist at least weekly and participates in personal prayer or meditation daily. She would choose to teach religion even if her contract did not require it.

At this point it is worth mentioning some observations that otherwise might go unnoticed. Not all lay teachers of religion are Catholic—over 3% are non-Catholic. Of the total number of lay teachers, over 7% are converts to the Catholic faith. When examining the race of the teachers, whites/others predominate. Slightly less than 3% are Hispanics, approximately 2% are blacks/non-Hispanics, and Asians/Pacific Islanders account for less than 1%. Less than 5% of lay teachers are men.

This picture of Catholic school teachers is quite different from what it was in 1965, when 65% of the teachers in Catholic elementary schools were members of religious congregations or were diocesan priests. Today, only 11% of teachers have such an affiliation, and, of this number, 82% are over age 45 (54% are over age 55!). This change in the composition of teachers in Catholic schools has many wide-ranging implications for Catholic education. The religious that remain teaching in Catholic schools are for the most part highly qualified to do the work they have undertaken. Their experience of religious education in their own formative years and their number of college and graduate credits in theology make them well prepared to teach religion. The numbers reported in this study demonstrate that religious are strongly dedicated to the devotional and ritual aspects of their faith.

Most current-day teachers of religion have a unique perspective of the Church that is inherently different from the majority of teachers a generation ago. Whereas most of the teachers in the 1960s had lived within the culture of religious communities, it may be appropriate to describe the teachers of today as enveloped in the culture of the family. Each group has an experience of the Church, but one that is different. The implication here is that the priorities and mundane obligations of these two groups are different, and one can rightly expect that the wealth of experiences they bring to their classrooms are also varied. How each group views and lives its faith influences its understanding and, in turn, its presentation of the Church and its teachings. This is a cataclysmic shift, and its meaning for the future of religious education cannot be understated. Each group has a language and a set of experiences that are invaluable to the formation and realization of a principle or idea. The transmission of religious faith is in the hands of a new group of artisans, and this means that the future of religion and even of theology itself will be reshaped because of this shift. It will be an understanding of God and Church that derives from the everyday lived experiences of people who approach life less theoretically and more practically.

Attitudes Toward Overall Teaching and Teaching Religion

Teachers seem to be more satisfied with their overall teaching qualifications, overall enjoyment, and overall accomplishments than with any of these aspects when related to the teaching of religion. Most (89%) of the lay teachers are generally satisfied with the faith difference they have made in the lives of their students; however, the satisfied outnumber the very satisfied by more than 2 to 1. When it comes to aspects of religion, teachers seem more prone to be satisfied rather than very satisfied. Table 6 indicates the degree of satisfaction teachers have with their qualifications, enjoyment, and accomplishments in the areas of overall teaching and the teaching of religion.

Table 6: Opinions of Teachers on Teaching in General and Teaching Religion

	% Laity	% Religious
Qualifications to teach in general		
Very satisfied	71.5	72.1
Satisfied	27.1	25.8
Unsatisfied	1.0	1.4
Very unsatisfied	0.1	0.3
Enjoyment of teaching overall		
Very satisfied	69.7	74.9
Satisfied	28.8	23.0
Unsatisfied	1.0	1.7
Very unsatisfied	0.2	0.0
Students' achievement in overall learning		
Very satisfied	34.8	28.9
Satisfied	61.6	66.6
Unsatisfied	3.1	3.8
Very unsatisfied	0.2	0.0
Sense of accomplishment in overall teaching		
Very satisfied	51.0	47.4
Satisfied	47.1	49.8
Unsatisfied	1.4	1.7
Very unsatisfied	0.0	0.3

(table continues)

	% Laity	% Religious
Qualifications to teach religion		
Very satisfied	31.5	72.8
Satisfied	57.0	25.4
Unsatisfied	9.6	1.4
Very unsatisfied	1.0	0.0
Enjoyment of teaching religion		
Very satisfied	49.3	77.0
Satisfied	44.0	21.3
Unsatisfied	5.2	1.4
Very unsatisfied	0.8	0.3
Difference made in faith life of students		
Very satisfied	26.2	34.1
Satisfied	63.0	55.7
Unsatisfied	8.9	7.7
Very unsatisfied	0.3	0.3
Sense of accomplishment in teaching religion		
Very satisfied	30.4	39.7
Satisfied	58.2	49.8
Unsatisfied	10.3	9.8
Very unsatisfied	0.6	0.0
Students' achievement in learning religion		
Very satisfied	26.5	29.3
Satisfied	65.0	61.7
Unsatisfied	7.6	8.4
Very unsatisfied	0.2	0.0
Knowledge of Church teachings		
Very satisfied	21.2	48.8
Satisfied	63.5	47.7
Unsatisfied	14.3	3.5
Very unsatisfied	0.5	0.0

Religious are twice as satisfied as lay teachers are with their qualifications to teach religion and their knowledge of Church teachings. Religious are more likely than lay teachers to enjoy teaching religion. In their satisfaction with teaching in general, lay and religious teachers' responses show little difference.

Religious Atmosphere

Table 7 illustrates that over four fifths of the lay teachers are satisfied with their personal devotional life and their sense of community among faculty. The table also lists regular opportunities that faculty members have for spiritual support.

Table 7: Religious Issues and Practices of Teachers		
	% Laity	**% Religious**
Personal devotional life		
Very satisfied	34.0	60.6
Satisfied	57.9	5.9
Unsatisfied	6.6	3.1
Very unsatisfied	0.4	0.0
Sense of faith community in school		
Very satisfied	30.8	33.1
Satisfied	53.3	56.1
Unsatisfied	14.0	10.8
Very unsatisfied	1.6	0.0
Actively encourage vocations to priesthood and religious life		
Strongly disagree	4.3	0.7
Disagree	43.7	16.0
Agree	45.0	58.2
Strongly agree	6.0	24.0
Faculty prays together regularly		
Yes	82.5	75.3
No	17.5	24.0
Faculty retreats provided regularly		
Yes	48.5	53.3
No	51.3	46.3
Religious updating provided regularly		
Yes	75.6	82.6
No	22.6	12.9
Opportunities for Eucharist provided regularly		
Yes	89.3	93.7
No	10.2	6.3
Opportunities for reconciliation provided regularly		
Yes	58.4	64.8
No	41.1	35.2

Teachers were asked to use their own judgment with regard to what they felt was a "regular" basis. Over four fifths of the lay teachers say the faculty prays together regularly, and about 9 out of 10 say that Eucharist is made available regularly. About half the teachers indicate that faculty retreats and opportunities for reconciliation are made available on a regular basis.

Generally, religious tend to be much more satisfied with their devotional life than are lay teachers. While over 80% of religious encourage vocations to the priesthood and religious life, only about 50% of the lay teachers do so.

Teaching Efficacy

In the Stark and Glock (1968) description of the dimensions of religiosity, the consequential dimension describes those things that people ought to do based upon what they believe. For John M. Finney (1978), the consequential dimension has more to do with religion's effects than with anything inherently religious. From the perspective of the Catholic Church, a comparable concept would be the desire of the catechist to see the faith engendered in the life of the student. As the then Bishop Bernardin (1974) stated, teachers of religion must be concerned about the personal growth in faith of their students. This is what Christian education is all about.

There are several different approaches one could use to assess the consequential dimension. In this study, the method employed was to examine the teachers' self-assessment of their overall teaching (three questions) and of their ability to influence the faith life of their students (three questions). The data in Table 8 present, therefore, the teachers' responses about their sense of efficacy.

Table 8: Opinions of Teachers on Teaching Efficacy

	% Laity	% Religious
A teacher really can't do much to help a student's <u>overall learning</u> because most of a student's motivation and performance depend on his or her home environment.		
Strongly disagree	14.1	13.2
Disagree	66.0	52.3
Agree	16.9	25.4
Strongly agree	3.0	8.7

(table continues)

	% Laity	% Religious
If I really try hard when I'm <u>teaching in general</u>, I can get through to even the most difficult or unmotivated students.		
Strongly disagree	1.0	0.3
Disagree	16.8	19.5
Agree	66.3	64.5
Strongly agree	15.8	15.3
A teacher really can't do much to help a student's <u>knowledge</u> because most of a student's motivation and performance depend on his or her home environment.		
Strongly disagree	19.1	13.2
Disagree	72.0	67.6
Agree	7.4	14.6
Strongly agree	1.4	3.5
If I really try hard when I'm <u>teaching about the Catholic faith</u>, I can get through to even the most difficult or unmotivated students.		
Strongly disagree	0.5	1.4
Disagree	20.1	41.1
Agree	66.3	45.3
Strongly agree	12.7	10.8
A teacher really can't do much to help a student's <u>practice of religion</u> because most of a student's motivation and performance depend on his or her home environment.		
Strongly disagree	4.1	2.8
Disagree	47.5	41.1
Agree	39.1	45.3
Strongly agree	9.1	10.8
If I really try hard, I can help a student improve his or her <u>practice of religion</u>, even with the most difficult or unmotivated student.		
Strongly disagree	1.0	2.1
Disagree	28.7	27.2
Agree	63.9	63.4
Strongly agree	5.9	6.3

Efficacy, according to Albert Bandura (1982), is best assessed by the teachers themselves. In this study, and in the literature in general, it seems that a teacher's sense of efficacy is strongly related to the assessment the teacher makes of student achievement. This scale is the standard efficacy measure used in teacher efficacy and has high reliability. Many of the major findings in the field of teacher efficacy are corroborated by this study. Of a highest possible score of 12 for each of the two efficacy scales used, the average score for religion-teaching efficacy is 8.14 and for overall-teaching efficacy, 8.97. These statistics and those that follow are for lay teachers of religion (Catholic and non-Catholic) only.

The set of variables that offered the greatest ability to predict efficacy were those dealing with teacher opinion (see Table 6). For religion-teaching efficacy these variables predicted 13% of the variance and 7% for overall-teaching efficacy. The major predictors were student achievement in religion, the difference that a teacher makes in the faith life of the student, a teacher's enjoyment of teaching religion, a teacher's enjoyment of overall teaching, and the sense of community among the faculty that a teacher experiences. This last predictor agrees with the research of Lee, Dedrick, and Smith (1991), who concluded that community is a strong predictor of efficacy.

The predictors for overall-teaching efficacy were a teacher's sense of overall accomplishment, a teacher's sense of overall enjoyment in teaching, the student's overall achievement, and the difference that a teacher makes in the faith life of the student.

Among the strongest predictors in this survey for both religion-teaching efficacy and overall-teaching efficacy was the teacher's assessment of student achievement. This result supports the finding of Ashton et al. (1983) that teachers' sense of efficacy is significantly related to student achievement. Another observation that the faith difference that a teacher makes in the life of the student is a predictor for both measures of efficacy.

With respect to religion-teaching efficacy, the higher the grade level, the less efficacious a teacher feels. This pattern is the inverse of that for knowledge and belief, where the higher the grade level, the higher the score. It is a common finding among researchers that those who teach lower grades have a greater sense of efficacy. This inverse relationship between knowledge and belief raises the issue of the relationship between these two. There is a very low correlation between religion-teaching efficacy and knowledge ($r = -.046$) and personal belief ($r = .035$). This information, along with the behavior of several of the predictors—those that were strong in predicting knowledge and personal belief had no such power with respect to religion-teaching efficacy and vice versa—suggests that knowledge of the subject matter is not tied directly to the sense of efficacy that a teacher feels with respect to teaching religion. In short, efficacy is not a measure of knowledge and belief nor do these in turn predict efficacy. This means that merely providing more information about the subject matter will not increase a teacher's sense of efficacy. There are other areas that should be examined.

The teachers' ages and whether they are certified or not make no difference in their sense of efficacy in teaching religion.

When teachers were asked about their qualifications to teach religion, the information given tended to be an important indicator of their sense of efficacy. The more satisfied the teacher is, the higher the efficacy score. This also holds true for teachers' sense of accomplishment in teaching religion and their personal assessment of their knowledge of Church teachings.

As is true with knowledge and personal belief, with efficacy in teaching religion, if a teacher had the option to teach or not teach religion, those who would opt to teach score higher. Two other variables that assisted in indicating teachers who score high in religion-teaching efficacy were a teacher's self-assessment of his or her personal devotional life (the more satisfied, the higher the score) and whether or not a teacher encourages vocations (those who encourage vocations score higher). Consideration of these issues may aid in faculty development. If teachers are not feeling efficacious about religious instruction, then certain areas may be pinpointed for examination, which may help them ameliorate their sense of religion-teaching efficacy.

Development of the Christian Lifestyle in Students

Another way of examining Stark and Glock's (1968) consequential dimension in the religiosity model is to examine how teachers teach and what they expect their students to do as a result of what they have been taught. Table 9 shows the results of such an examination among the lay and religious teachers in this study.

Table 9: Teaching Methods and Teachers' Expectations of Their Students

	% Laity	% Religious
1. It is important that my religion students		
A. understand the teachings of the Church.	31.1	28.2
B. believe the teachings of the Church.	7.9	8.7
C. act on the teachings of the Church.	60.8	62.0

(table continues)

	% Laity	% Religious
2. For me, the most important objective in the religion courses I teach is that my students		
A. respond to life's situations in Christian ways.	89.4	86.8
B. are able to express confidence in their beliefs.	4.4	5.2
C. understand why they believe.	5.9	7.0
3. The greatest goal my students can achieve is		
A. knowledge of the faith.	3.0	2.8
B. the ability to live in Christian ways.	73.5	70.0
C. trust in God.	23.4	26.5
4. I consider myself to have been most successful if my students		
A. become trusting individuals.	7.6	8.4
B. are convicted about the beliefs of their faith.	26.8	35.2
C. become more involved in helping others.	65.2	54.0
5. In my religion class preparations, I feel it is most important		
A. to make sure that Church teachings are presented accurately.	12.4	20.2
B. to suggest opportunities and ways that one's faith can be lived.	71.0	58.2
C. to develop a sense of trust in God.	16.2	20.6
6. I am doing my best job teaching religion		
A. when I emphasize involvement in the community.	13.8	9.4
B. when I clearly identify what makes someone a Christian.	36.5	30.7
C. if I can develop within my students a trusting reliance in God.	49.1	59.9
7. Faith, as I present it, is best associated with		
A. believing.	35.8	41.8
B. trusting.	19.0	20.2
C. doing.	44.7	37.6

(table continues)

	% Laity	% Religious
8. I judge my students to be most successful when their faith is exhibited as		
A. knowledge.	1.5	6.3
B. practice.	32.5	41.5
C. action.	65.6	57.8
9. If and when I use the Bible in my classes, it is primarily		
A. to let students read about their faith from a firsthand source.	18.8	10.5
B. to allow students to become familiar with the mystery of God's actions.	15.5	41.5
C. to let students experience stories of how faith causes people to act.	65.3	47.0
10. In teaching religion, I find the lesson to be most effective for the students when I		
A. challenge them to have confidence in their faith.	13.4	24.0
B. give examples of how people live out their faith.	68.9	57.5
C. mention or discuss important issues of the day.	17.0	16.7

The purpose of this section in the survey was to ascertain the aspect from which a catechist primarily operates. The underpinning notion here, as explained in chapter 2, is that the teaching of religion has three major divisions: the affective, the behavioral, and the cognitive. (A description of these dimensions can be found in two major works: Thomas Groome's [1980] *Christian Religious Education: Sharing Our Story and Vision* and a document by the United States Catholic Conference [1972], *To Teach as Jesus Did.*) Each aspect calls forth different responses from an individual: affect calls forth trust; behavior, action; and cognition, knowledge. Each of the 10 questions in this section of the survey had three responses reflecting these three aspects of the teaching of religion.

The 10 questions were of two types: process and outcome. Processes are the methods or approaches that a teacher uses in the teaching of religion, and outcomes are the desired results that a teacher wishes to see in his or her students.

Questions 1, 2, 3, 4, and 8 dealt with the student as recipient and questions 5, 6, 7, 9, and 10 dealt with the teacher as actor. When the first set is examined one finds that a behavioral response is highly preferred by lay teachers to either an affective or a cognitive response (70.9% versus 15.2% and 13.7%); likewise by religious teachers (66.7% versus 18.1% and 15.9%). With the teacher as actor, the preference for a behavioral response is not as dramatic, although it is still much more likely than either the affective or the cognitive (52.7% versus 22.6% and 24.3% for lay teachers and 41.9% versus 33.2% and 23.9% for religious teachers).

What does all this mean? The emphasis in the process and outcomes of religion is heavily sided towards a behavioral mode when contrasted with the affective and the cognitive. In their written responses that accompanied the survey, many teachers found this to be the most difficult section of the instrument because of the forced choices they were asked to make. Many teachers responded that they do not make such divisions when they teach religion; rather, they consider all three aspects to be equally important.

CHAPTER FOUR

Findings

Knowlege and Beliefs

In this section, the teachers' responses to 25 issues dealing with their knowledge and personal beliefs are examined. The issues are divided into four areas: general Christian teachings, Catholic Church discipline, Catholic morality, and teachings particular to the Catholic view of Christianity. In the succeeding pages, each survey item is examined in the following manner:

1. The issue is presented as a topical heading and is followed by a set of related statements in a brief table. This table shows the percentages of all teachers (i.e., religious, lay Catholic, and non-Catholic) who chose one of the statements listed under that issue. The teachers were asked to identify the statement that "comes closest to the Church's position" and then the statement "that comes closest to my [i.e., the teacher's] personal position."

2. A second table compares the different response rates for lay Catholics, religious, and non-Catholics. Four positions are examined: (a) those who know the Church's position, (b) those who believe the Church's position as their own, (c) those who know and believe the Church's position, and (d) those who do not know or believe the Church's position.

3. A commentary on the issue provides the documentation used to validate the Church's position and includes some highlights of the statistical data listed in the tables. The two major sources for the documentation are the *Enchiridion Symbolorum Definitionum et Declarationium* (Denzinger-Schönmetzer) and the *1983 Code of Canon Law* (Can.), although other sources are also cited.

4. A third table shows percentages of responses, for Catholic lay teachers of religion only, in these six categories: know the Church's position (*know*); believe the Church's position (*believe*); know and believe the Church's position (*know and believe*); know but do not believe the Church's position (*know but do not believe*); do not know and do not believe the Church's position (*do not know or believe*); and do not know but believe the Church's position (*do not know but believe*). These categories are divided among four

background characteristics of the teachers: method of certification, preparation for certification, age, and number of years of religious education.

Reading the commentary can become tedious because of the constant use of the words "know" and "believe" and their various forms. To ameliorate this problem, when a specific category is mentioned, its title is italicized, as in item 4 immediately above.

Issues of General Christian Teaching

For these four issues (listed under Section II of the questionnaire as no. 1, God's existence; no. 2, divinity of Jesus; no. 14, existence of the devil; and no. 15, Resurrection), all percentages of teachers are high in both the knowledge and belief categories.

In general, these issues are the most recognized and the most believed. The only issue, by comparison, that is not as strong as the others is the one about the existence of the devil. Slightly more than 11% believe the devil is as powerful as God, and 9% believe the devil does not exist. Nonetheless, it appears that Catholic lay teachers are generally knowing and believing Christians in that they know and believe the basic Christian teachings.

GOD'S EXISTENCE

Statement	% of all teachers	
	Identify as closest to Church's position	Identify as closest to personal position
A. God is a supreme, omnipotent Being.	**99.8**	**97.8**
B. God is fallible and subject to change.	0.2	1.8
C. God does not exist.	0.0	0.3

Comparison of Percentages of Teacher Responses about Their Knowledge of and Belief in the Church's Position

Teachers	Know	Believe	Know and believe	Do not know or believe
Catholic laity	100	98	98	0
Religious	100	99	99	0
Non-Catholics	100	93	93	0

Commentary. Denzinger-Schönmetzer (no. 3001) from Vatican I (1870) — "The holy, Catholic Roman Church believes and confesses: There is one God, true and living, Creator and Lord of heaven and earth, mighty, eternal, immense, incomprehensible, infinite in His intellect and will and in all perfection."

This is the statement with the greatest percentages of *know* and *believe*. In each group, over 90% of the teachers *know and believe* the Church's position.

Percentages of Catholic Lay Teachers' Responses about Their Knowledge of and Belief in the Church's Position by Background Characteristics

Background characteristic	Know	Believe	Know and believe	Know but do not believe	Do not know or believe	Do not know but believe
Method of Certification						
None	100	95	95	5	0	<1
Informal	100	97	97	3	0	0
Formal (non-college)	100	98	98	2	0	0
Formal (college)	100	99	99	1	0	0
Preparation for Certification						
College	100	99	99	1	0	0
Diocese	100	98	98	2	0	0
Attending	100	97	97	3	0	0
No program	100	98	98	2	0	0
Age						
Under 25	99	98	97	2	0	0
25-34	100	96	96	4	0	0
35-44	100	97	97	3	0	0
45-54	100	99	99	1	0	0
55 or older	100	100	100	0	0	0
Years of Religious Education						
None	99	97	97	2	<1	<1
1-4	99	96	96	4	0	<1
5-8	100	97	97	3	0	0
9-12	100	97	97	3	0	0
12+	100	99	99	1	0	0

DIVINITY OF JESUS

	% of all teachers	
Statement	Identify as closest to Church's position	Identify as closest to personal position
A. Jesus is fully human and fully divine.	**94.0**	**92.0**
B. Jesus, being fully divine, only had the appearance of a human.	5.3	6.0
C. Jesus was human and then adopted as God's Son.	0.3	0.7
D. Jesus was not divine, but a very holy human.	0.0	0.9

Comparison of Percentages of Teacher Responses about Their Knowledge of and Belief in the Church's Position

Teachers	Know	Believe	Know and believe	Do not know or believe
Catholic laity	94	92	91	6
Religious	100	99	99	0
Non-Catholics	88	84	83	11

Commentary. Denzinger-Schönmetzer (no. 253) from the Council of Ephesus (431)—"If anyone does not confess that the Word who is from God the Father has been united to the flesh according to the hypostasis and that Christ is one with His own flesh, that is to say that the same is at once God and man, may he be cursed."

Over 80% of all groups *know and believe* the Church's position. Approximately 10% of lay teachers with no religious education, of those under age 35, and of those with no preparation to teach religion fall in the *do not know or believe* category.

Percentages of Catholic Lay Teachers' Responses about Their Knowledge of and Belief in the Church's Position by Background Characteristics

Background characteristic	Know	Believe	Know and believe	Know but do not believe	Do not know or believe	Do not know but believe
Method of Certification						
None	89	86	85	5	10	1
Informal	92	89	88	4	7	1
Formal (non-college)	95	93	92	2	5	<1
Formal (college)	97	96	96	2	2	0
Preparation for Certification						
College	94	93	91	3	5	1
Diocese	95	93	92	3	5	0
Attending	93	91	90	3	7	1
No program	91	89	88	4	8	1
Age						
Under 25	89	82	82	8	10	1
25-34	89	87	85	4	10	2
35-44	95	92	92	3	5	0
45-54	96	95	94	2	3	0
55 or older	96	97	96	0	3	1
Years of Religious Education						
None	88	87	86	2	11	1
1-4	92	90	88	4	7	2
5-8	91	89	89	2	9	<1
9-12	93	90	89	4	6	1
12+	96	94	94	2	3	<1

EXISTENCE OF THE DEVIL

Statement	% of all teachers	
	Identify as closest to Church's position	Identify as closest to personal position
A. The devil is not as powerful as God.	**84.4**	**78.2**
B. The devil is as powerful as God.	12.6	11.5
C. The devil is more powerful than God.	0.1	0.5
D. The devil does not exist.	2.0	9.0

Comparison of Percentages of Teacher Responses about Their Knowledge of and Belief in the Church's Position

Teachers	Know	Believe	Know and believe	Do not know or believe
Catholic laity	84	77	75	14
Religious	93	91	89	6
Non-Catholics	75	63	57	19

Commentary. Denzinger-Schönmetzer (no. 402) from the Council of Braga (561)—In this series of statements, the Church affirms that the devil is inferior to God. It affirms the biblical account that the devil was at one time a good angel.

Only 58% of lay teachers under age 25 *know and believe* the Church's position. This percentage is low when compared to the other observed groups. Nearly 20% of this group *know but do not believe* the Church's position. Approximately 10% of all groups in religious education *know but do not believe* the Church's position, with younger teachers more likely than older ones to do so.

Percentages of Catholic Lay Teachers' Responses about Their Knowledge of and Belief in the Church's Position by Background Characteristics

Background characteristic	Know	Believe	Know and believe	Know but do not believe	Do not know or believe	Do not know but believe
Method of Certification						
None	100	95	95	5	0	<1
Informal	100	97	97	3	0	0
Formal (non-college)	100	98	98	2	0	0
Formal (college)	100	99	99	1	0	0
Preparation for Certification						
College	84	79	77	7	14	3
Diocese	84	79	76	8	13	3
Attending	85	78	76	9	13	2
No program	81	72	69	12	17	2
Age						
Under 25	77	61	58	19	20	3
25-34	81	73	70	11	16	3
35-44	83	76	74	9	16	2
45-54	87	82	80	7	11	2
55 or older	87	85	82	5	10	4
Years of Religious Education						
None	78	73	68	10	17	6
1-4	78	71	68	10	20	2
5-8	79	73	70	9	19	3
9-12	84	76	74	10	14	2
12+	87	81	79	8	11	2

RESURRECTION

Statement	% of all teachers	
	Identify as closest to Church's position	Identify as closest to personal position
A. Jesus rose bodily from the dead.	**94.6**	**88.2**
B. Jesus rose only in spirit from the dead.	5.2	11.0
C. Jesus did not rise from the dead.	0.2	0.3

Comparison of Percentages of Teacher Responses about Their Knowledge of and Belief in the Church's Position

Teachers	Know	Believe	Know and believe	Do not know or believe
Catholic laity	94	88	88	5
Religious	99	96	96	1
Non-Catholics	95	88	88	5

Commentary. Denzinger-Schönmetzer (nos. 791, 801, and 852)—The Fourth Lateran Council (1215) and the Second General Council of Lyons (1274) clarify the Church's position that Christ rose bodily ("in carne") from the dead.

Over 85% of all groups *know and believe* the Church's position. About 10% of lay teachers with no formal religious preparation for certification *know but do not believe* the Church's position. The same is true for those under age 35. Twelve percent of lay teachers under age 25 *do not know or believe* the Church's position.

Percentages of Catholic Lay Teachers' Responses about Their Knowledge of and Belief in the Church's Position by Background Characteristics

Background characteristic	Know	Believe	Know and believe	Know but do not believe	Do not know or believe	Do not know but believe
Method of Certification						
None	90	79	78	12	10	<1
Informal	94	85	85	9	6	0
Formal (non-college)	95	89	89	6	5	0
Formal (college)	97	94	94	4	3	0
Preparation for Certification						
College	97	91	91	6	3	0
Diocese	95	89	89	6	5	0
Attending	94	87	87	8	6	0
No program	92	84	84	9	7	0
Age						
Under 25	89	77	77	12	12	0
25-34	91	81	81	10	9	0
35-44	95	89	89	6	5	0
45-54	96	92	92	5	4	0
55 or older	98	94	94	4	2	0
Years of Religious Education						
None	93	83	82	11	6	<1
1-4	92	86	86	6	8	0
5-8	93	84	84	9	7	0
9-12	94	86	86	8	6	0
12+	96	91	91	5	4	0

Issues of Catholic Church Discipline

There are four issues in this section, listed in the questionnaire as priesthood (no. 5), marriage (no. 19), reception of Communion (no. 24), and sacrament of penance (no. 25). What is distinctive about these issues is that in the hierarchy of truths, they derive the force of their authority from Church law and are considered as matters of discipline.

None of these issues has the recognition nor the acceptance among teachers of religion that the issues of general Christian teaching do. Even though two of the issues, priesthood and marriage, receive high scores in the area of knowledge, they do not receive nearly as high scores in the area of belief. For each issue, over 30% of those who know the Church's position do not personally hold it.

Two of the issues, reception of Communion and reception of penance, receive low scores in both knowledge and belief. As regards the reception of Communion, Catholic lay teachers are more likely to identify and believe a position that is more restrictive than the Church's stance. On the other hand, with penance, they generally identify a more restrictive position as the Church's teaching, but their belief is evenly distributed among three views: the Church's position, one that is more restrictive, and one that is less restrictive.

PRIESTHOOD

Statement	% of all teachers	
	Identify as closest to Church's position	Identify as closest to personal position
A. Only men can be priests and only men can assist on the altar in celebrating the Eucharist.	2.0	3.6
B. Only men can be priests and deacons, but other ministries may be open to men and women.	**72.1**	**38.1**
C. Only men can be priests, but the diaconate and other ministries may be open to men and women.	6.6	15.3
D. Priesthood and all other ministries can be open to both men and women.	1.1	42.3

Comparison of Percentages of Teacher Responses about Their Knowledge of and Belief in the Church's Position

Teachers	Know	Believe	Know and believe	Do not know or believe
Catholic laity	73	38	33	23
Religious	76	48	45	21
Non-Catholics	41	18	15	55

Commentary. Can. 1024 and 230—"Only a baptized male validly receives sacred ordination." "Lay persons can fulfill the function of lector during liturgical actions by temporary deputation; likewise all lay persons can fulfill the functions of commentator or cantor or other functions, in accord with the norm of law."

Over 33% of all groups *know but do not believe* the Church's position. Only those lay teachers with formal college training for certification are more likely *to know and believe* rather than *know but do not believe*.

Thirty percent of lay teachers with no certification *do not know or believe* the Church's position. Lay teachers are more likely to *know and believe* (33%) rather than *not know or believe* (23%); however, overall, they *know but do not believe* (40%). Over 50% of non-Catholics *do not know or believe* the Church's position.

Percentages of Catholic Lay Teachers' Responses about Their Knowledge of and Belief in the Church's Position by Background Characteristics

Background characteristic	Know	Believe	Know and believe	Know but do not believe	Do not know or believe	Do not know but believe
Method of Certification						
None	62	36	28	34	30	7
Informal	71	33	30	42	26	3
Formal (non-college)	75	40	36	40	21	4
Formal (college)	72	43	39	34	24	4

(table continues)

Background characteristic	Know	Believe	Know and believe	Know but do not believe	Do not know or believe	Do not know but believe
Preparation for Certification						
College	72	36	31	41	23	5
Diocese	73	38	33	40	23	4
Attending	75	40	36	39	21	4
No program	7	36	31	40	25	5
Age						
Under 25	70	36	30	40	24	6
25-34	74	41	37	37	21	4
35-44	69	34	29	41	26	5
45-54	76	36	34	42	22	2
55 or older	74	44	37	36	20	6
Years of Religious Education						
None	66	33	31	35	32	2
1-4	71	38	34	38	24	5
5-8	73	39	32	42	20	7
9-12	73	37	32	41	23	5
12+	74	38	35	39	23	4

MARRIAGE

	% of all teachers	
Statement	Identify as closest to Church's position	Identify as closest to personal position
A. Under no circumstances, except for the death of a spouse, may a Catholic enter into a second marriage.	8.1	4.7
B. Under no circumstances, except for the death of a spouse or where an annulment or dissolution has been granted, may a Catholic enter into a second marriage.	**89.3**	**58.5**
C. A Catholic may enter into a second marriage if either of the spouses in the first marriage commits adultery.	0.4	0.9
D. A Catholic may enter into a second marriage if either of the spouses in the first marriage commits adultery or if there is physical or emotional abuse.	1.1	19.6
E. Incompatibility in the first marriage would allow a Catholic to enter into a second marriage.	0.8	14.8

Comparison of Percentages of Teacher Responses about Their Knowledge of and Belief in the Church's Position

Teachers	Know	Believe	Know and believe	Do not know or believe
Catholic laity	90	57	55	9
Religious	93	77	76	6
Non-Catholics	70	28	25	28

Commentary. Can. 1141, 1142, and 1143—These canons state the Church's position that only death can dissolve a marriage that is ratified and consummated. There are certain privileges (Pauline and Petrine) that allow for the dissolution of marriages in particular cases. An annulment is the recognition by the Church that a marriage was not valid from the start because certain elements were missing.

Overall, teachers are more likely to *know and believe* the Church's position, but the number of those who *know but do not believe* is large. As regards method of preparation, lay teachers with no preparation or informal preparation are as likely to *know and believe* as to *know but do not believe*, while those with either type of formal education are more than twice as likely to *know and believe* as to *know but do not believe*. A similar comparison can be made for the age and years of religious education variables. Lay teachers who are older or have more religious education are much more likely to *know and believe* the Church's position than are those who are younger or have little religious education. Nearly one sixth of those with no preparation to teach religion as well as of those with no religious education *do not know or believe* the Church's position.

Percentages of Catholic Lay Teachers' Responses about Their Knowledge of and Belief in the Church's Position by Background Characteristics

Background characteristic	Know	Believe	Know and believe	Know but do not believe	Do not know or believe	Do not know but believe
Method of Certification						
None	80	40	38	42	17	3
Informal	87	51	49	38	11	2
Formal (non-college)	92	61	60	32	7	1
Formal (college)	91	69	67	24	7	2
Preparation for Certification						
College	89	61	58	31	7	3
Diocese	91	60	58	33	8	2
Attending	90	57	56	35	9	1
No program	87	50	49	38	12	2

(table continues)

Background characteristic	Know	Believe	Know and believe	Know but do not believe	Do not know or believe	Do not know but believe
Age						
Under 25	83	49	44	39	12	5
25-34	87	48	46	41	12	2
35-44	90	52	52	39	9	<1
45-54	92	66	64	28	6	2
55 or older	91	73	71	20	8	2
Years of Religious Education						
None	82	48	46	37	16	2
1-4	80	56	49	31	1	7
5-8	90	52	50	40	9	2
9-12	89	53	52	37	10	1
12+	93	64	63	30	6	1

RECEPTION OF COMMUNION

	% of all teachers	
Statement	Identify as closest to Church's position	Identify as closest to personal position
A. Only Catholics can receive the Eucharist at a Catholic service.	78.4	48.1
B. Only Catholics and those who believe in real presence may receive the Eucharist at a Catholic service.	**17.6**	**29.9**
C. Any Christian may receive the Eucharist at a Catholic service.	3.4	16.0
D. Anyone who wishes may receive the Eucharist at a Catholic service.	0.3	5.4

Comparison of Percentages of Teacher Responses about Their Knowledge of and Belief in the Church's Position

Teachers	Know	Believe	Know and believe	Do not know or believe
Catholic laity	17	30	13	67
Religious	19	38	16	59
Non-Catholics	18	30	14	66

Commentary. "Decree on Ecumenism" of the Second Vatican Council (1964a)—In a series of commentaries, the Church has clarified who may receive Communion. Those from Eastern Christian rites who have valid orders may receive Catholic Communion without question. Those from Protestant or Anglican faiths must hold the faith that the Catholic Church herself professes concerning the Eucharist, and that they are unable to approach a minister of their own confession. This permission is determined on a particular individual basis and not in a blanket sense.

Less than 20% of all respondents were able to identify the Church's position (i.e., *know*). Lay teachers who are more likely to do so are those who have formal college courses for their certification (21%) and those over age 55 (23%). Both of these groups are the most likely to *believe* the Church's position (34% and 39%, respectively).

The low response rate in the area of knowledge by all groups indicates that there are difficulties with this question, maybe with the terminology, the selection options in the question, or the issue itself.

Percentages of Catholic Lay Teachers' Responses about Their Knowledge of and Belief in the Church's Position by Background Characteristics

Background characteristic	Know	Believe	Know and believe	Know but do not believe	Do not know or believe	Do not know but believe
Method of Certification						
None	13	21	9	4	75	12
Informal	16	26	11	5	69	15
Formal (non-college)	18	32	14	4	64	18
Formal (college)	21	34	17	4	62	17
Preparation for Certification						
College	21	34	17	4	62	17
Diocese	18	31	14	5	65	17
Attending	16	31	13	3	66	18
No program	15	23	11	4	73	12

(table continues)

Background characteristic	Know	Believe	Know and believe	Know but do not believe	Do not know or believe	Do not know but believe
Age						
Under 25	12	19	9	3	79	9
25-34	13	26	9	4	70	17
35-44	18	28	13	4	68	15
45-54	19	32	14	4	64	18
55 or older	23	39	21	3	58	18
Years of Religious Education						
None	18	23	13	5	72	11
1-4	17	34	14	2	64	19
5-8	16	28	13	3	69	15
9-12	17	27	13	4	69	14
12+	18	32	14	4	64	18

SACRAMENT OF PENANCE

	% of all teachers	
Statement	Identify as closest to Church's position	Identify as closest to personal position
A. In order for any sin to be forgiven, a Catholic must receive the sacrament of penance.	36.1	13.8
B. A Catholic must receive the sacrament of penance once a year even if he or she has committed only minor (venial) sins.	42.7	29.5
C. It is necessary to receive the Sacrament of Penance only if a Catholic has committed mortal sins.	**20.2**	**26.7**
D. There is no need for a Sacrament of Penance because God knows our sins and only God can forgive them.	0.4	26.2
E. There is no need for the Sacrament of Penance because sins are between the individual person and the one offended.	0.0	2.6

Comparison of Percentages of Teacher Responses about Their Knowledge of and Belief in the Church's Position

Teachers	Know	Believe	Know and believe	Do not know or believe
Catholic laity	18	25	13	71
Religious	44	49	40	47
Non-Catholics	6	7	5	92

Commentary. Can. 920 and 989—Canon 920 states that a Catholic must receive Communion once a year, preferably during the Easter season. Canon 989 states: "After having attained the age of discretion, each of the faithful is bound by an obligation faithfully to confess *serious sins* at least once a year." If one does not have serious sin, one does not *have to* go to confession.

Less than 5% of lay teachers under age 25 *know* or *believe* the Church's position. Seven percent of those between ages 25 and 34 *know* the Church's position and 12% *believe* it. The disparity between religious and Catholic laity is twofold as regards knowledge. Those with formal college preparation for certification are 5 times more likely to *know* the Church's position and 4 times more likely to *believe* it than those with no preparation. The number of years of religious education is also a strong predictor of knowledge and belief.

Percentages of Catholic Lay Teachers' Responses about Their Knowledge of and Belief in the Church's Position by Background Characteristics

Background characteristic	Know	Believe	Know and believe	Know but do not believe	Do not know or believe	Do not know but believe
Method of Certification						
None	6	9	4	2	89	5
Informal	12	18	9	3	79	9
Formal (non-college)	23	30	17	6	65	13
Formal (college)	31	39	26	5	57	13
Preparation for Certification						
College	21	33	17	5	63	16
Diocese	23	30	17	5	65	12
Attending	12	18	8	4	78	10
No program	11	15	7	4	81	8

(table continues)

Background characteristic	Know	Believe	Know and believe	Know but do not believe	Do not know or believe	Do not know but believe
Age						
Under 25	3	4	2	2	95	2
25-34	7	12	3	4	84	8
35-44	17	23	12	5	73	11
45-54	25	35	19	6	60	15
55 or older	29	41	26	3	56	15
Years of Religious Education						
None	10	17	7	3	80	10
1-4	14	16	8	6	78	8
5-8	79	22	21	58	20	<1
9-12	77	26	25	53	22	<1
12+	76	35	34	43	23	1

Issues of Catholic Morality

In this section there are five issues, which are listed under Section II of the survey as no. 10, elective abortion; no. 12, artificial birth control; no. 20, euthanasia; no. 21, discrimination; and no. 23, premarital sex.

Three of these issues have a disparity of over 30% between teachers who know the Church's position and those who believe it. The highest rate of rejection of the Church's position is in birth control: 66% of teachers who know the Church's position do not hold it. About 50% of the teachers do not consider artificial birth control morally wrong. Abortion also has a relatively high rejection rate, although a further analysis demonstrates that less than 15% of the teachers believe abortion on demand to be morally permissible. Most teachers endorse a restricted view of abortion, with 30% accepting the Church's position.

Although 64% of the teachers accept the Church's position on premarital sexual relations, about 15% think premarital sexual relations is not morally wrong. Among all the moral issues, this one has the highest rate of recognition. The Church's position on euthanasia is not readily recognized by many lay teachers of religion, but more than 50% of them hold it. When the more restrictive position is considered here, both knowledge and belief are recognized and accepted by over 90% of the teachers. The vast majority of teachers know and believe the Church's position on discrimination.

ELECTIVE ABORTION

	% of all teachers	
Statement	Identify as closest to Church's position	Identify as closest to personal position
A. Direct elective abortion is wrong in all situations.	**77.1**	**30.3**
B. Direct elective abortion is wrong except to save the life of the mother.	18.7	22.4
C. Direct elective abortion is wrong except to save the life of the mother and in cases of rape or incest.	4.0	32.0
D. Direct elective abortion is an individual's right under most circumstances.	0.0	13.8

Comparison of Percentages of Teacher Responses about Their Knowledge of and Belief in the Church's Position

Teachers	Know	Believe	Know and believe	Do not know or believe
Catholic laity	77	28	27	22
Religious	75	55	54	25
Non-Catholics	82	16	15	17

Commentary. "Declaration on Abortion" by Paul VI (1974); "Pastoral Constitution on the Church in the Modern World" from the Second Vatican Council (1965d, nos. 27 and 51)—Direct abortion is always wrong. Indirect abortion, however, may be permissible under the principle of the double effect. Indirect abortion occurs as a consequence of a medical treatment or surgical operation to save the life of the mother that results in the regrettable but unavoidable death of the fetus. It is never permitted, however, to directly choose to elect an abortion under any circumstances.

Although only about one third of the teachers agree with the position that comes closest to the Church's stance, over half of the teachers select the more restricted view of abortion. Less than one sixth hold an unrestricted view of abortion.

A breakdown of the various groups reveals that lay teachers with formal college preparation are twice as likely to *believe* the Church's position as are those with no preparation. The same comparison can be made for teachers over age 55 age and those under age 25. This same relationship exists not only for those who *believe*, but also for those who *know and believe*: The more years of religious education teachers have had, the more likely they are to *believe* the Church's position as their own. Approximately one fifth of all lay teachers in each group *do not know or believe* the Church's position; slightly more *know and believe* what the Church teaches.

This is the only issue for which non-Catholics outscored the other two groups in knowledge of the Church's position, and non-Catholics were the smallest group in the *do not know or believe* category.

Percentages of Catholic Lay Teachers' Responses about Their Knowledge of and Belief in the Church's Position by Background Characteristics

Background characteristic	Know	Believe	Know and believe	Know but do not believe	Do not know or believe	Do not know but believe
Method of Certification						
None	79	21	20	59	20	1
Informal	79	25	24	56	20	1
Formal (non-college)	75	28	27	47	24	1
Formal (college)	77	43	43	34	22	<1
Preparation for Certification						
College	75	30	29	46	24	1
Diocese	78	32	31	47	22	<1
Attending	77	22	22	55	22	1
No program	78	24	23	55	21	1
Age						
Under 25	80	20	18	62	18	2
25-34	80	21	20	60	19	1
35-44	78	25	25	53	22	0
45-54	73	33	32	41	26	1
55 or older	78	40	39	39	21	1
Years of Religious Education						
None	78	15	14	64	21	<1
1-4	78	22	22	57	22	0
5-8	79	22	21	58	20	<1
9-12	77	26	25	53	22	<1
12+	76	35	34	43	23	1

ARTIFICIAL BIRTH CONTROL

Statement	% of all teachers	
	Identify as closest to Church's position	Identify as closest to personal position
A. Artificial birth control is never appropriate in marriage.	**80.7**	**14.1**
B. Artificial birth control is appropriate only when the wife's health is endangered.	14.1	13.1
C. Artificial birth control is permissible in marriage as long as the couple does have the intention to have children at some point in time.	2.4	20.7
D. Artificial birth control is not morally wrong.	2.0	50.5

Comparison of Percentages of Teacher Responses about Their Knowledge of and Belief in the Church's Position

Teachers	Know	Believe	Know and believe	Do not know or believe
Catholic laity	81	11	11	19
Religious	80	42	42	20
Non-Catholics	75	5	6	24

Commentary. "Humanae Vitae" of Paul VI (1968, no. 11)—"Each and every marital act must of necessity retain its intrinsic relationship to the procreation of human life."

This issue holds the greatest rejection rate among the issues surveyed —the differential between the knowledge and belief is 66%. Lay teachers with formal college preparation are more likely to *know and believe* the Church's position than are those who are age 55 or older. Approximately two thirds of each group know the Church's position but do not hold it personally (i.e., *know but do not believe*).

Percentages of Catholic Lay Teachers' Responses about Their Knowledge of and Belief in the Church's Position by Background Characteristics

Background characteristic	Know	Believe	Know and believe	Know but do not believe	Do not know or believe	Do not know but believe
Method of Certification						
None	81	6	6	75	19	<1
Informal	83	9	9	73	18	0
Formal (non-college)	79	14	13	66	20	<1
Formal (college)	81	23	23	58	19	0
Preparation for Certification						
College	79	11	11	69	20	0
Diocese	82	13	12	69	18	0
Attending	82	9	9	73	18	0
None	80	8	8	72	20	0
Age						
Under 25	81	8	8	73	19	0
25-34	81	8	8	74	19	0
35-44	82	9	9	73	18	0
45-54	81	10	10	71	19	0
55 or older	80	26	25	55	19	1
Years of Religious Education						
None	83	10	10	73	17	0
1-4	84	11	11	73	16	0
5-8	77	11	11	67	23	0
9-12	82	7	7	75	18	0
12+	80	14	14	67	19	0

EUTHANASIA

Statement	% of all teachers	
	Identify as closest to Church's position	Identify as closest to personal position
A. Dying people should always be provided needed nutrition.	60.9	36.5
B. Dying people should always be provided needed nutrition except when to do so would involve an extraordinary means of preserving life.	**37.4**	**54.7**
C. Dying people should always be provided needed nutrition except for those in great pain.	0.4	2.2
D. Dying people should always be provided needed nutrition except for those whose quality of life has been lessened.	0.3	5.2

Comparison of Percentages of Teacher Responses about Their Knowledge of and Belief in the Church's Position

Teachers	Know	Believe	Know and believe	Do not know or believe
Catholic laity	35	53	32	44
Religious	63	70	62	29
Non-Catholics	18	36	13	59

Commentary. "Declaration on Euthanasia" by the Congregation for the Doctrine of the Faith (1980) and *Nutrition and Hydration: Moral and Pastoral Reflections* by the United States Catholic Conference (1992, no. 6)—"It is our considered judgment that while legitimate Catholic moral debate continues, decisions about these patients should be guided by a presumption in favor of medically assisted nutrition and hydration. A decision to discontinue such measures should be made in light of a careful assessment of the burdens and benefits of nutrition and hydration for the individual patient and his or her family and community."

More teachers hold the Church's position personally than are able to identify it as the Church's position. Lay teachers with formal college preparation are more than twice as likely as those with no preparation to *know and believe* the Church's position. The same is true for lay teachers over age 45 and those under age 34 and for teachers with over 12 years of religious education and those with no religious education. Between 35% and 61% of all groups of lay teachers *do not know or believe* the Church's position.

Percentages of Catholic Lay Teachers' Responses about Their Knowledge of and Belief in the Church's Position by Background Characteristics

Background characteristic	Know	Believe	Know and believe	Know but do not believe	Do not know or believe	Do not know but believe
Method of Certification						
None	22	46	19	3	51	27
Informal	28	48	25	3	49	23
Formal (non-college)	38	56	35	3	41	21
Formal (college)	54	63	51	2	35	12
Preparation for Certification						
College	41	55	39	3	43	16
Diocese	40	58	37	3	40	20
Attending	28	51	25	3	46	26
No program	27	46	24	4	50	23
Age						
Under 25	22	39	19	3	58	21
25-34	23	44	18	5	51	26
35-44	29	54	27	3	43	28
45-54	47	61	44	2	37	16
55 or older	51	60	49	2	38	11
Years of Religious Education						
None	18	43	16	2	55	28
1-4	21	38	20	1	61	18
5-8	29	52	25	4	45	26
9-12	31	53	27	4	44	25
12+	46	59	43	3	38	16

DISCRIMINATION

Statement	% of all teachers	
	Identify as closest to Church's position	Identify as closest to personal position
A. All people deserve equal opportunity.	**96.9**	**93.9**
B. Some people deserve equal opportunity while others must earn it.	0.3	0.5
C. All people must earn equal opportunity.	1.4	4.7
D. Not all people deserve equal opportunity.	1.1	0.5

Comparison of Percentages of Teacher Responses about Their Knowledge of and Belief in the Church's Position

Teachers	Know	Believe	Know and believe	Do not know or believe
Catholic laity	97	94	92	1
Religious	97	97	96	2
Non-Catholics	89	94	86	2

Commentary. "Declaration on the Relation of the Church to Non-Christian Religions" (no. 5) from the Second Vatican Council (1965b)—"We cannot truly pray to God the Father of all if we treat any people in other than brotherly fashion, for all men are created in God's image. . . . There is no basis therefore, either in theory or in practice for any discrimination between individual and individual, or between people and people arising either from human dignity or from the rights which flow from it."

This is the only item in this group of moral issues on which the overwhelming majority *know and believe* the Church's position.

Percentages of Catholic Lay Teachers' Responses about Their Knowledge of and Belief in the Church's Position by Background Characteristics

Background characteristic	Know	Believe	Know and believe	Know but do not believe	Do not know or believe	Do not know but believe
Method of Certification						
None	95	90	87	8	2	3
Informal	96	93	91	5	2	2
Formal (non-college)	97	94	93	5	2	1
Formal (college)	98	97	95	2	1	1
Preparation for Certification						
College	98	96	94	3	<1	2
Diocese	97	93	92	5	2	1
Attending	98	93	91	6	1	2
No program	97	94	92	5	<1	3
Age						
Under 25	95	93	89	7	0	5
25-34	95	92	90	6	2	3
35-44	99	94	93	6	<1	<1
45-54	97	94	93	4	2	1
55 or older	97	94	94	4	3	0
Years of Religious Education						
None	95	92	90	5	4	1
1-4	97	95	93	4	<1	2
5-8	97	93	91	6	2	2
9-12	97	92	91	6	2	2
12+	98	95	94	4	1	1

PREMARITAL SEX

Statement	% of all teachers	
	Identify as closest to Church's position	Identify as closest to personal position
A. Premarital sex is always morally wrong.	**99.0**	**61.4**
B. Premarital sex is permissible when the couple is engaged.	0.3	12.0
C. Premarital sex is permissible after a couple has been dating for a period of time.	0.0	6.9
D. Premarital sex is not morally wrong.	0.3	15.0

Comparison of Percentages of Teacher Responses about Their Knowledge of and Belief in the Church's Position

Teachers	Know	Believe	Know and believe	Do not know or believe
Catholic laity	99	61	61	1
Religious	99	91	91	1
Non-Catholics	95	60	58	2

Commentary. *Casti Connubii* of Pius XI (1930)—In this encyclical letter, the pope confirmed the Church's long-standing tradition that sexual intercourse is appropriate only to the married state and to perform the sexual act outside of marriage is to do something that is intrinsically evil.

Very few of the teachers do not *know* the Church's position here. The important contrasts here are between those who *know and believe* and those who *know but do not believe.* Of lay teachers with no certification, more do not believe the Church's position than do; however, of teachers with formal college certification, 3 times as many are more likely to believe the Church's position. Those with preparation for certification through the diocese are twice as likely to believe the Church's position.

Age offers some of the most dramatic contrasts. Lay teachers under age 34 are much more likely not to believe the Church's position, and those over 35 are more likely to believe it (especially those over age 55, who are 5 times more likely to believe the Church's position than not believe it). One aberration from this trend is found in the area of years of religious education. Almost identical numbers exist for teachers with 4 or fewer years of religious education and those with 9 years or more. In all the other groups, *know and believe* is higher than *know but do not believe*.

Percentages of Catholic Lay Teachers' Responses about Their Knowledge of and Belief in the Church's Position by Background Characteristics

Background characteristic	Know	Believe	Know and believe	Know but do not believe	Do not know or believe	Do not know but believe
Method of Certification						
None	100	44	44	56	<1	0
Informal	100	56	56	44	<1	0
Formal (non-college)	99	67	67	32	1	0
Formal (college)	99	77	76	23	<1	0
Preparation for Certification						
College	100	57	57	43	0	0
Diocese	99	67	67	32	1	0
Attending	99	58	58	41	1	0
No program	100	52	52	48	0	0
Age						
Under 25	100	35	35	65	0	0
25-34	100	42	42	58	0	0
35-44	99	57	57	42	<1	0
45-54	99	76	76	23	1	0
55 or older	99	84	84	15	<1	0
Years of Religious Education						
None	99	63	63	37	<1	0
1-4	98	61	61	37	2	0
5-8	100	55	55	45	0	0
9-12	99	58	58	41	<1	0
12+	99	65	65	35	1	0

Issues Particular to the Catholic View of Christianity

There are 12 issues in this section, which are presented in Section II of the questionnaire as follows: requirements for salvation (no. 3), Eucharistic presence (no. 4), Bible (no. 6), hierarchy of the Church (no. 7), afterlife (no. 8), infallibility of the pope (no. 9), Church moral teaching (no. 11), role of Mary (no. 13), predestination (no. 16), salvation (no. 17), suffering in the world (no. 18), and homosexuality (no. 22). What distinguishes the items in this section is that they are issues on which Catholics differ from other Christian religions. Among these 12 items, Eucharistic presence is the only one with a relatively high difference between teachers' knowledge and belief. Twenty percent of those who know the Church's position do not believe it. On the positive side, over 66% of the teachers know and believe the Church's position; but, with an issue so central to the Catholic Christian view of Christianity, this does not seem to be a sufficient number.

There are three issues on which the teachers are most likely to not know or believe the Church's position: authorship of the Bible, infallibility of the pope, and whether God predestines people. The relatively even spread of the responses for knowledge and belief suggests that teachers are just as likely to choose one position as another. In neither the knowledge nor the belief category is the Church's position the one most frequently chosen. This is not the case with the issue of infallibility of the pope, where the Church's stance is the most chosen response among the options available; nonetheless, in both knowledge and belief, teachers are more likely to choose a position that is not that of the Church. Concerning predestination, teachers are nearly as likely to choose the Church's position for knowledge and belief as not to choose it.

There are four issues on which a majority of the teachers know and believe the Church's position: the role of faith and good works in salvation, the existence of an afterlife, the role of Mary in salvation, and the role of suffering in human existence. Over 75% of all teachers know and believe the Church's position on each of these issues (only 73% of lay teachers know and believe the Church's position on Mary).

There are four issues on which the teachers are more likely to believe than to know the Church's position: the establishment of the hierarchy of the Church, the role of Church teaching in making a moral decision, who can be saved, and the participation of homosexuals in the life of the Church. Teachers overwhelmingly choose the Church's position and one that is more restrictive with respect to the establishment of the hierarchy of the Church. Although they are slightly more likely to recognize the Church's position on these two, they are 4 times more likely to believe it (versus the more restrictive position).

Only one third of the teachers can identify the Church's stance on the role of Church teaching in making a moral decision. Nearly two thirds identify the most restrictive position as the Church's. With respect to belief, however, over two thirds choose the Church's position as their own.

As regards who can be saved, the Church's position is most likely to be chosen among the available options; however, teachers are 20% more likely to believe the Church's stance than to identify it as a teaching of the Church. The same is true for the issue of teaching about homosexuals and the Church, with 30% of the teachers being more likely to believe the Church's position than to identify it.

REQUIREMENTS FOR SALVATION

	% of all teachers	
Statement	Identify as closest to Church's position	Identify as closest to personal position
A. Only faith is necessary for salvation.	10.5	7.1
B. Only good works are necessary for salvation.	0.5	1.9
C. Both faith and good works are necessary for salvation.	**88.1**	**89.5**
D. Neither faith nor good works are necessary for salvation.	0.5	1.0

Comparison of Percentages of Teacher Responses about Their Knowledge of and Belief in the Church's Position

Teachers	Know	Believe	Know and believe	Do not know or believe
Catholic laity	88	89	84	7
Religious	95	95	93	3
Non-Catholics	80	74	64	11

Commentary. Denzinger-Schönmetzer (nos. 1559, 1560, and 1561) from the Council of Trent (1547)—These articles from the "Decree on Justification" confirm that the Church believes that both faith and good works are necessary in order to be saved. This statement was to counter the position of Protestants in the Reformation which held that faith alone was necessary for salvation.

The vast majority of teachers in all groups *know and believe* the Church's position; even nearly three quarters of non-Catholics *believe* the Church's teaching in this area.

Percentages of Catholic Lay Teachers' Responses about Their Knowledge of and Belief in the Church's Position by Background Characteristics

Background characteristic	Know	Believe	Know and believe	Know but do not believe	Do not know or believe	Do not know but believe
Method of Certification						
None	84	84	77	8	9	7
Informal	88	89	84	3	8	4
Formal (non-college)	87	90	84	3	7	7
Formal (college)	92	92	89	3	5	3
Preparation for Certification						
College	91	92	87	4	4	5
Diocese	88	90	85	3	7	5
Attending	87	89	83	4	7	6
No program	86	87	82	4	10	4
Age						
Under 25	86	88	81	5	7	7
25-34	87	87	82	4	8	5
35-44	87	91	85	2	7	6
45-54	89	91	86	4	6	5
55 or older	87	89	85	3	9	4
Years of Religious Education						
None	82	86	78	4	11	8
1-4	85	85	81	4	11	4
5-8	86	87	80	5	8	7
9-12	88	91	85	3	6	6
12+	89	90	86	3	7	4

EUCHARISTIC PRESENCE

Statement	% of all teachers	
	Identify as closest to Church's position	Identify as closest to personal position
A. The bread and wine really and truly become the Body and Blood of Christ at Mass.	**87.8**	**67.2**
B. The bread and wine change only in spiritual presence at the Mass.	10.3	24.8
C. The bread and wine take on only a commemorative presence (memorial) at the Mass.	1.5	6.7
D. No change happens to the bread and wine at Mass.	0.0	0.4

Comparison of Percentages of Teacher Responses about Their Knowledge of and Belief in the Church's Position

Teachers	Know	Believe	Know and believe	Do not know or believe
Catholic laity	87	65	65	13
Religious	99	96	96	1
Non-Catholics	80	31	30	19

Commentary. Denzinger-Schönmetzer (no. 1636) from the Council of Trent (1551)—"The holy Council teaches and openly and straightforwardly professes that in the blessed sacrament of the holy Eucharist, after the consecration of the bread and wine, our Lord Jesus Christ, true God and man, is truly, really and substantially contained under the appearances of those perceptible realities."

Twenty percent of the teachers, even though they know the Church's position, do not hold it personally (i.e., *know but do not believe*). Examining lay teachers' method of certification reveals that less than 50% of those with no preparation *know and believe* the Church's position, and 84% of those with formal college training *know and believe*. Twenty-five percent of lay teachers with no preparation for certification *know but do not believe* the Church's position. Thirty-two percent of those under age 34 *know but do not believe* in the real presence, while less than 10% of those over 55 years old *know but do not believe.* Method of certification and age are two important predictors of belief in the real presence.

Percentages of Catholic Lay Teachers' Responses about Their Knowledge of and Belief in the Church's Position by Background Characteristics

Background characteristic	Know	Believe	Know and believe	Know but do not believe	Do not know or believe	Do not know but believe
Method of Certification						
None	78	46	46	31	23	0
Informal	84	57	57	27	16	0
Formal (non-college)	90	69	69	20	10	0
Formal (college)	94	84	84	10	6	0
Preparation for Certification						
College	88	68	68	20	12	<1
Diocese	90	70	69	20	10	0
Attending	83	59	59	24	17	0
No program	84	59	59	25	16	0
Age						
Under 25	72	42	42	31	27	0
25-34	81	49	49	32	19	0
35-44	88	64	64	24	12	0
45-54	91	75	75	17	9	0
55 or older	92	84	84	8	8	0
Years of Religious Education						
None	82	59	59	24	17	<1
1-4	81	58	58	23	19	0
5-8	82	54	54	27	18	0
9-12	86	62	62	25	14	0
12+	90	72	72	18	10	0

BIBLE

| | % of all teachers | |
Statement	Identify as closest to Church's position	Identify as closest to personal position
A. The authorship of the Bible is solely divine.	34.9	16.8
B. The authorship is primarily divine with some human influence.	26.3	33.4
C. The authorship of the Bible is fully divine and fully human.	**24.1**	**24.8**
D. The authorship is primarily human with some divine influence.	11.3	19.4
E. The authorship of the Bible is solely human.	2.1	4.6

Comparison of Percentages of Teacher Responses about Their Knowledge of and Belief in the Church's Position

Teachers	Know	Believe	Know and believe	Do not know or believe
Catholic laity	25	25	20	70
Religious	21	22	19	76
Non-Catholics	21	24	15	70

Commentary. "Dogmatic Constitution on Divine Revelation" (paragraph 11) of the Second Vatican Council (1965c)—This document states that God made full use of human authors in the writing of the Bible, and so the Word of God is like Jesus, fully human and fully divine.

The evenness of the spread among the responses suggests that teachers are not well-informed about the Church's teaching on the authorship of the Bible. This is the only issue on which younger teachers are more likely to identify the Church's position, even though ever so slightly, than are older teachers. This may be due to the influence of a document of Pope Pius XII (1943), *Divino Afflante Spiritu*, which stressed the divine authorship of the Bible against Scripture scholars who were challenging the Bible's divine nature. This document served as the basis for the Church's teachings in the years immediately preceding the Second Vatican Council. Over two thirds of all groups *do not know or believe* the Church's position.

Percentages of Catholic Lay Teachers' Responses about Their Knowledge of and Belief in the Church's Position by Background Characteristics

Background characteristic	Know	Believe	Know and believe	Know but do not believe	Do not know or believe	Do not know but believe
Method of Certification						
None	21	24	16	5	72	8
Informal	26	26	19	7	68	6
Formal (non-college)	24	24	19	5	71	5
Formal (college)	23	25	21	3	72	4
Preparation for Certification						
College	24	25	18	6	69	7
Diocese	23	24	18	5	72	5
Attending	26	26	21	6	68	6
No program	27	28	21	5	67	6
Age						
Under 25	26	25	19	7	68	6
25-34	27	29	23	5	66	7
35-44	25	25	19	6	69	7
45-54	23	22	17	6	73	4
55 or older	23	25	22	1	74	3
Years of Religious Education						
None	23	29	18	5	66	11
1-4	25	29	20	5	65	10
5-8	27	24	20	7	69	4
9-12	25	25	19	6	69	6
12+	24	25	20	4	71	5

HIERARCHY OF THE CHURCH

| | % of all teachers | |
Statement	Identify as closest to Church's position	Identify as closest to personal position
A. The episcopal and priestly structure of the Church was divinely instituted by Jesus and has remained the same since Jesus' time.	36.8	14.3
B. The episcopal and priestly structure of the Church was divinely instituted by Jesus and affected by human institution.	**48.3**	**60.3**
C. The current episcopal and priestly structure of the Church was not instituted by Jesus but was guided over time by the Holy Spirit.	12.0	13.6
D. The episcopal and priestly structure of the Church is purely a human institution.	1.8	10.5

Comparison of Percentages of Teacher Responses about Their Knowledge of and Belief in the Church's Position

Teachers	Know	Believe	Know and believe	Do not know or believe
Catholic laity	49	62	42	31
Religious	45	53	38	40
Non-Catholics	45	48	31	39

Commentary. Denzinger-Schönmetzer (no. 3053) from Vatican I (1870) and "Dogmatic Constitution on the Church" (paragraphs 18-20) of the Second Vatican Council (1964b)—Both of these documents confirm that the Church was divinely instituted by Jesus and that the Church has appointed other ministers to help in the carrying out of its mission to proclaim the Gospel.

Teachers are more likely to personally *believe* the Church's position than to identify it. Among the several breakdowns, teachers are as likely to *know and believe* as they are to *not know or believe*. This is the only issue on which lay Catholic religion teachers are more likely to *know* and to *believe* the Church's position than are either of the two other groups.

Percentages of Catholic Lay Teachers' Responses about Their Knowledge of and Belief in the Church's Position by Background Characteristics

Background characteristic	Know	Believe	Know and believe	Know but do not believe	Do not know or believe	Do not know but believe
Method of Certification						
None	45	59	36	8	33	23
Informal	49	61	42	7	32	19
Formal (non-college)	50	62	42	8	31	19
Formal (college)	46	58	40	6	35	18
Preparation for Certification						
College	49	61	39	10	30	21
Diocese	48	61	41	7	32	20
Attending	51	61	44	7	32	17
No program	48	64	42	6	30	22
Age						
Under 25	53	62	43	10	29	19
25-34	54	67	47	7	26	20
35-44	47	62	39	8	31	22
45-54	45	60	40	6	35	20
55 or older	50	56	43	7	37	13
Years of Religious Education						
None	44	52	33	11	37	19
1-4	49	59	44	5	36	15
5-8	52	61	43	9	30	18
9-12	51	64	44	7	29	20
12+	47	62	41	6	32	21

AFTERLIFE

Statement	% of all teachers	
	Identify as closest to Church's position	Identify as closest to personal position
A. All people eventually go to heaven.	10.6	17.7
B. All people immediately go to heaven because hell does not exist.	0.5	2.2
C. It is truly possible for people to go to heaven or to hell.	**88.0**	**78.2**
D. There is no heaven or hell.	0.1	1.0

Comparison of Percentages of Teacher Responses about Their Knowledge of and Belief in the Church's Position

Teachers	Know	Believe	Know and believe	Do not know or believe
Catholic laity	88	77	75	10
Religious	96	88	87	3
Non-Catholics	76	78	63	8

Commentary. Denzinger-Schönmetzer (no. 411) of the Council of Constantinople (543) and Denzinger-Schönmetzer (no. 76)—The first of these citations condemns the belief that eventually all people go to heaven. The second is the Athanasian Creed, which states that "those who have done good will go to eternal life, but those who have done evil to eternal fire."

Older lay teachers are more likely to *know and believe* the Church's position than are the younger ones. Among those who *do not know or believe* the Church's position are teachers who are younger and those with little religious education. Overall, they are twice as likely to *not know or believe*.

Percentages of Catholic Lay Teachers' Responses about Their Knowledge of and Belief in the Church's Position by Background Characteristics

Background characteristic	Know	Believe	Know and believe	Know but do not believe	Do not know or believe	Do not know but believe
Method of Certification						
None	83	75	70	13	12	5
Informal	83	73	69	14	13	4
Formal (non-college)	90	80	79	11	9	1
Formal (college)	93	83	81	12	5	2
Preparation for Certification						
College	90	79	75	15	6	5
Diocese	89	79	77	12	9	2
Attending	85	74	71	14	13	3
No program	86	75	72	14	12	3
Age						
Under 25	74	66	61	13	21	5
25-34	82	73	69	13	14	4
35-44	89	78	75	14	9	2
45-54	92	80	79	13	8	1
55 or older	91	81	81	11	8	<1
Years of Religious Education						
None	77	66	63	14	20	3
1-4	78	70	65	13	17	5
5-8	89	77	76	13	9	2
9-12	88	78	76	12	10	3
12+	91	79	78	13	8	1

INFALLIBILITY OF THE POPE

	% of all teachers	
Statement	Identify as closest to Church's position	Identify as closest to personal position
A. The Pope is infallible in all matters.	26.7	8.1
B. The Pope is infallible in all matters regarding the Church only.	25.7	24.9
C. The Pope is infallible in matters of faith and morals only.	**40.4**	**38.4**
D. The Pope can never claim infallibility.	5.7	26.4

Comparison of Percentages of Teacher Responses about Their Knowledge of and Belief in the Church's Position

Teachers	Know	Believe	Know and believe	Do not know or believe
Catholic laity	36	34	27	58
Religious	85	80	78	13
Non-Catholics	11	16	8	82

Commentary. Denzinger-Schönmetzer (no. 3074) from Vatican I (1870)— This citation states that when the pope speaks *ex cathedra* (i.e., officially and with the intention of making a definitive statement) about issues of faith and morals, this teaching is to be accepted as infallible.

Well over 50% of all teachers *do not know or believe* the Church's position. The two notable exceptions here are those with formal college certification to teach and those over age 55. Only 9% of those under age 25 *know and believe* the Church's position. Teachers with over 12 years of religious education are more than twice as likely as those with less than 4 years to *know and believe* the Church's view.

Percentages of Catholic Lay Teachers' Responses about Their Knowledge of and Belief in the Church's Position by Background Characteristics

Background characteristic	Know	Believe	Know and believe	Know but do not believe	Do not know or believe	Do not know but believe
Method of Certification						
None	23	21	14	9	70	7
Informal	25	24	18	7	69	6
Formal (non-college)	40	40	32	8	53	8
Formal (college)	66	60	56	10	30	4
Preparation for Certification						
College	45	40	35	10	50	5
Diocese	40	39	32	9	53	7
Attending	28	28	20	8	64	8
No program	28	26	21	8	66	6
Age						
Under 25	19	16	9	10	74	8
25-34	18	17	11	7	77	6
35-44	29	30	21	8	62	9
45-54	51	45	40	11	44	5
55 or older	62	60	54	8	32	6
Years of Religious Education						
None	19	28	14	5	67	14
1-4	21	22	14	7	72	7
5-8	23	24	18	5	71	6
9-12	31	29	22	8	63	7
12+	50	44	39	11	45	5

CHURCH MORAL TEACHING

Statement	% of all teachers	
	Identify as closest to Church's position	Identify as closest to personal position
A. People must accept everything the Church teaches about morals at all times.	62.0	14.8
B. People must accept everything the Church teaches about morals except in particular circumstances.	4.6	8.0
C. Church teaching is an essential component in a moral decision.	**32.3**	**69.6**
D. Church teaching is merely an opinion on a particular issue.	0.2	6.7

Comparison of Percentages of Teacher Responses about Their Knowledge of and Belief in the Church's Position

Teachers	Know	Believe	Know and believe	Do not know or believe
Catholic laity	31	71	28	26
Religious	45	63	43	35
Non-Catholics	22	63	21	36

Commentary. Can. 752—"A religious respect of intellect and will, even if not the assent of faith, is to be paid to the teaching which the Supreme Pontiff or the college of bishops enunciate on faith or morals when they exercise the authentic Magisterium even if they do not intend to proclaim it with a definitive act; therefore the Christian faithful are to take care to avoid whatever is not in harmony with that teaching."

Lay teachers over 55 years old are twice as likely as those under age 25 to *know and believe* the Church's position. The more formal the method of certification, the less likely the lay teacher is to *believe* the Church's position. Although most teachers do *not know but believe* the Church's position, a significant proportion of teachers *know and believe* as well as *do not know or believe*. This is the only issue on which a higher percentage of lay Catholic teachers are more likely to *believe* the Church's position than are members of religious congregations. One third of the religious *do not know or believe* the Church's position.

Percentages of Catholic Lay Teachers' Responses about Their Knowledge of and Belief in the Church's Position by Background Characteristics

Background characteristic	Know	Believe	Know and believe	Know but do not believe	Do not know or believe	Do not know but believe
Method of Certification						
None	25	66	20	5	29	45
Informal	28	71	25	4	25	46
Formal (non-college)	35	71	32	2	27	39
Formal (college)	36	67	34	2	31	33
Preparation for Certification						
College	26	66	25	2	32	42
Diocese	32	70	30	3	27	40
Attending	33	69	28	5	25	41
No program	29	76	26	3	21	50
Age						
Under 25	26	64	19	7	29	45
25-34	27	72	23	4	23	49
35-44	28	74	25	3	24	48
45-54	36	71	33	3	27	38
55 or older	39	64	38	1	35	26
Years of Religious Education						
None	30	69	28	3	28	42
1-4	25	71	23	1	28	47
5-8	28	69	24	4	27	45
9-12	31	73	27	4	24	46
12+	34	70	31	3	28	38

ROLE OF MARY

| | % of all teachers | |
Statement	Identify as closest to Church's position	Identify as closest to personal position
A. Mary's role in our salvation is as important as the role of Jesus.	16.3	12.9
B. Mary's role in salvation is unique, distinct from that of Jesus and the saints.	**80.2**	**78.1**
C. Mary's role in salvation is the same as other saints.	2.0	4.7
D. Mary has no special role in salvation.	1.0	4.0

Comparison of Percentages of Teacher Responses about Their Knowledge of and Belief in the Church's Position

Teachers	Know	Believe	Know and believe	Do not know or believe
Catholic laity	80	78	73	15
Religious	87	86	85	12
Non-Catholics	65	45	37	28

Commentary. "Dogmatic Constitution on the Church" (nos. 62 and 66) from the Second Vatican Council (1964b)—"Therefore the Blessed Virgin is invoked in the Church under the titles of Advocate, Helper, Benefactress, and Mediatrix. This, however, is so understood that it neither takes away anything from nor adds anything to the dignity and efficacy of Christ the Mediator." "Mary has by grace been exalted above all angels and men to a place second only to her Son. . . ."

In almost all areas, teachers are as likely to *know*, to *believe*, and to *know and believe* the Church's position.

Percentages of Catholic Lay Teachers' Responses about Their Knowledge of and Belief in the Church's Position by Background Characteristics

Background characteristic	Know	Believe	Know and believe	Know but do not believe	Do not know or believe	Do not know but believe
Method of Certification						
None	71	71	63	8	21	8
Informal	78	77	71	8	16	6
Formal (non-college)	83	80	77	6	14	3
Formal (college)	81	78	75	6	16	3
Preparation for Certification						
College	77	76	70	7	17	6
Diocese	81	79	74	6	15	4
Attending	81	80	75	6	15	5
No program	79	78	73	7	16	5
Age						
Under 25	74	77	69	5	18	9
25-34	72	74	65	7	19	9
35-44	81	78	73	8	14	4
45-54	85	82	79	5	13	2
55 or older	84	82	80	4	14	2
Years of Religious Education						
None	71	70	62	9	20	9
1-4	74	73	68	6	21	5
5-8	77	78	69	8	14	9
9-12	82	80	76	6	14	4
12+	82	80	76	6	14	4

SALVATION

| | % of all teachers | |
Statement	Identify as closest to Church's position	Identify as closest to personal position
A. Only those who believe in Jesus can attain heaven.	18.7	9.6
B. Only those who believe in God can attain heaven.	33.8	23.1
C. Anyone can attain heaven.	**46.0**	**66.0**

Comparison of Percentages of Teacher Responses about Their Knowledge of and Belief in the Church's Position

Teachers	Know	Believe	Know and believe	Do not know or believe
Catholic laity	45	66	45	34
Religious	62	74	62	26
Non-Catholics	21	39	19	60

Commentary. Denzinger-Schönmetzer (no. 3870) from a letter by the Holy Office (1949)—"To gain eternal salvation it is not always required that a person be incorporated in reality as a member of the Church, but it is required that he belongs to it at least in desire and longing. It is not always necessary that this desire be explicit, as it is with catechumens. When a man is invincibly ignorant, God also accepts an implicit desire, so called because it is contained in the good disposition of soul by which a man wants his will to be conformed to God's will."

Overall, teachers are more likely to *believe* the Church's position than to identify it as such. Lay teachers with no preparation to teach religion as well as those with less than 4 years of religious education are most likely to *not know or believe* the Church's position.

Percentages of Catholic Lay Teachers' Responses about Their Knowledge of and Belief in the Church's Position by Background Characteristics

Background characteristic	Know	Believe	Know and believe	Know but do not believe	Do not know or believe	Do not know but believe
Method of Certification						
None	34	58	34	0	42	24
Informal	39	61	39	<1	38	23
Formal (non-college)	50	69	49	0	31	10
Formal (college)	53	70	52	0	30	18
Preparation for Certification						
College	47	72	47	0	28	25
Diocese	48	68	48	0	32	21
Attending	41	62	41	0	37	22
No program	42	62	41	0	37	21
Age						
Under 25	39	65	39	<1	35	26
25-34	41	63	41	<1	37	22
35-44	45	66	45	0	34	21
45-54	46	70	46	0	30	24
55 or older	51	66	51	0	35	14
Years of Religious Education						
None	33	56	33	0	44	23
1-4	41	57	41	0	43	16
5-8	39	61	39	0	39	22
9-12	44	66	43	<1	34	23
12+	51	71	50	0	29	21

SUFFERING IN THE WORLD

Statement	% of all teachers	
	Identify as closest to Church's position	Identify as closest to personal position
A. God causes us to suffer for our benefit.	13.9	11.0
B. God does not intend suffering, but allows it.	**81.7**	**82.9**
C. God is powerless to prevent suffering.	3.6	5.3

Comparison of Percentages of Teacher Responses about Their Knowledge of and Belief in the Church's Position

Teachers	Know	Believe	Know and believe	Do not know or believe
Catholic laity	80	82	78	15
Religious	98	95	95	2
Non-Catholics	66	68	61	28

Commentary. Apostolic letter *Salvifici Doloris* of John Paul II (1984a)—In this document the pope presents the Church's position that God uses the suffering of man to bring about a better world. We are invited to share in the sufferings of Christ.

Teachers with no method of certification, who are younger, and who have less than 4 years of religious education are 2 to 3 times more likely to *not know or believe* the Church's position. The more formal the method of certification to teach religion, the more likely the teacher is to *know*, to *believe*, and to *know and believe* the Church's position.

Percentages of Catholic Lay Teachers' Responses about Their Knowledge of and Belief in the Church's Position by Background Characteristics

Background characteristic	Know	Believe	Know and believe	Know but do not believe	Do not know or believe	Do not know but believe
Method of Certification						
None	64	66	61	3	31	5
Informal	78	80	75	3	17	5
Formal (non-college)	83	85	81	3	12	5
Formal (college)	90	90	88	2	8	2
Preparation for Certification						
College	81	85	79	1	14	5
Diocese	83	84	81	3	13	4
Attending	80	81	77	3	17	4
No program	75	77	71	4	20	6
Age						
Under 25	64	62	59	5	33	3
25-34	71	74	67	4	22	7
35-44	81	82	78	3	15	4
45-54	87	89	85	2	10	4
55 or older	88	90	87	2	9	3
Years of Religious Education						
None	70	76	69	1	23	7
1-4	70	72	65	5	23	7
5-8	74	75	70	4	22	5
9-12	80	82	77	3	16	5
12+	86	87	84	2	11	3

HOMOSEXUALITY

	% of all teachers	
Statement	Identify as closest to Church's position	Identify as closest to personal position
A. Homosexuals by orientation are to be treated as outside the Church.	21.5	6.1
B. Homosexuals by orientation are to be treated as sinners in need of forgiveness and are not full members of the Church.	28.9	15.6
C. Homosexuals by orientation can be full members of the Church.	**46.2**	**75.3**

Comparison of Percentages of Teacher Responses about Their Knowledge of and Belief in the Church's Position

Teachers	Know	Believe	Know and believe	Do not know or believe
Catholic laity	44	75	43	1
Religious	71	84	70	1
Non-Catholics	23	63	21	2

Commentary. "Declaration on Certain Questions Concerning Sexual Ethics" (1975) and "Declaration on Homosexuals" from the Congregation for the Doctrine of the Faith (1986)—Both documents distinguish between homosexuals by orientation (or condition) and homosexual activities. All people, no matter what their sexual orientation, are called to live chaste lives. A person's orientation does not place him or her outside the Church.

Between 18% and 50% of all groups of lay teachers *do not know but believe* the Church's position. With respect to method of certification and age, the more formal the method and the older the teachers, the more likely they are to *know* the Church's position; but as regards *belief*, all groups are relatively the same.

Percentages of Catholic Lay Teachers' Responses about Their Knowledge of and Belief in the Church's Position by Background Characteristics

Background characteristic	Know	Believe	Know and believe	Know but do not believe	Do not know or believe	Do not know but believe
Method of Certification						
None	29	71	28	1	28	42
Informal	39	75	38	1	24	37
Formal (non-college)	48	74	47	1	25	27
Formal (college)	58	80	57	1	19	23
Preparation for Certification						
College	50	80	49	1	19	31
Diocese	48	76	47	1	23	29
Attending	36	70	35	1	29	36
No program	39	72	38	<1	27	34
Age						
Under 25	20	70	20	0	30	50
25-34	33	75	32	<1	24	43
35-44	43	75	42	1	24	33
45-54	52	73	50	1	25	23
55 or older	60	77	59	1	22	18
Years of Religious Education						
None	40	72	40	0	28	32
1-4	40	70	38	1	29	31
5-8	36	74	35	1	24	40
9-12	40	72	38	1	27	34
12+	51	78	50	<1	22	28 ·

General Commentary. Besides the four major divisions that have already been presented, there are four more divisions into which the 25 issues break down based upon the pattern of the responses of the teachers. They are (a) where a majority of the teachers know and believe what the Church teaches, (b) where a majority of the teachers do not know what the Church teaches but believe the Church teaching personally, (c) where a majority of the teachers know what the Church teaches but do not believe it (by at least 20%), and (d) where a majority of the teachers neither know nor believe what the Church teaches.

Issues in the division where a majority of the teachers *know and believe* the Church's position:

1. God's existence
2. Divinity of Jesus
3. Requirements for salvation
8. Afterlife
13. Role of Mary
14. Existence of the devil
15. Resurrection
18. Suffering in the world
21. Discrimination

Issues in the division where teachers are more likely to believe the Church's position than to know it (*do not know but believe*. At least 50% of the teachers believe the Church's position). The percentage given reflects the difference between knowledge and belief in favor of belief:

7. Hierarchy of the Church (12%)
11. Church moral teaching (37%)
17. Salvation (20%)
20. Euthanasia (18%)
22. Homosexuality (29%)

Issues in the division where a majority of teachers *know but do not believe* the Church's position. (At least 20% more teachers know the Church's position than hold it personally.) The percentage given reflects the difference between knowledge and belief in favor of knowledge:

4. Eucharistic presence (21%)
5. Priesthood (34%)
10. Elective abortion (47%)
12. Artificial birth control (67%)
19. Marriage (31%)
23. Premarital sex (35%)

Issues in the division where no clear consensus of the teachers is established for either knowing or believing (*do not know or believe*) the

Church's position (i.e., teachers are as likely to choose one response as another):

6. Bible
9. Infallibility of the pope
16. Predestination
24. Reception of communion
25. Sacrament of penance

The reasons behind these divisions are not known. There are certain trends, however, within each breakdown. Where teachers are most likely to *know and believe* the Church's position, the majority of the nine items listed are dogmatic in nature. All four of the issues regarding Christianity in general, four of the issues on the Catholic view of Christianity, and one of the issues on morality are found here. Where most teachers are likely to *not know but believe* the Church's position, four of the issues focus on the Catholic view of Christianity and one on morality. Where the majority of teachers know the Church's position but do not hold it personally (i.e., *know but do not believe*), of the six issues listed, three are moral issues, two are on Church discipline, and the other is on the Catholic view of Christianity. Lastly, where no clear consensus demonstrates that teachers know and believe the Church's position (i.e., *do not know or believe*), of these five issues, three deal with the Catholic view of Christianity and two with Church discipline.

CHAPTER FIVE

Conclusions

In the past 30 years a dramatic shift has taken place in the composition of Catholic elementary school teachers. In 1965, 65% of the teachers were members of religious congregations; in 1995, nearly 90% were members of the laity. With the present data, we now have the means to compose a picture of who is teaching religion in Catholic elementary schools, and we also can determine what is needed to help them.

Many of these lay teachers have grown up within the Church through their attendance at Catholic grade schools and high schools. Less than one quarter of the teachers have graduate course credits in theology, however, so they are dependent on the courses and preparation the Church provides to help them in their teaching of religion. Nonetheless, one fifth of all lay teachers are teaching religion without having undergone any certification and another fifth are teaching while attending courses. Teachers enjoy teaching religion, and more than four fifths would choose to teach religion even if it were not mandated by their contract.

The teachers' attitude toward teaching religion is generally quite positive, although somewhat less positive than their attitude toward teaching in general. Over 80% of the teachers are satisfied with the sense of a faith community in their school. Teachers also have a relatively strong sense of efficacy in their ability to make a difference in the faith life of their students.

A major section of the survey was dedicated to understanding what teachers know and believe about the teachings of the Church. This survey was not intended to be comprehensive nor to render some type of norm-referenced evaluation of the knowledge and beliefs of the teachers. The topics for the survey were derived from several sources that detail the core curriculum for Catholic Church catechists and for adult education within the Church. What is important about this survey is the format used. Teachers were not asked directly if they agree with the Church's position on a certain issue; rather, they were given a list of alternative statements and asked to choose which one came closest to representing the Church's teaching and then which one came closest to representing their personal belief. The benefit of this method is that the respondents could avoid giving favorable answers and avoid seeing the questions as a litmus test of their orthodoxy.

The issues, based upon the wording of the statements, fell into four distinct areas: general Christian dogma (beliefs that are held by Catholics and other mainline Christian faiths); Catholic Church discipline (issues that deal with juridical or canonical prescriptions); Catholic morality (issues on which the Catholic Church has taken a stance regarding their morality or immorality); and Catholic dogma (theological beliefs that are particular to Catholics alone and not other mainline Christian faiths).

The following chart shows average scores on these 25 items differ depending on the breakdown that is used to illustrate the results.

Percentages of Teachers' Responses about Their Knowledge of and Belief in Church Teachings

Issues	Religious		Laity		Non-Catholic	
	Know	Believe	Know	Believe	Know	Believe
Christian dogma	98	96	93	89	87	78
Catholic discipline	58	53	49	37	33	16
Catholic morality	83	71	78	49	72	42
Catholic dogma	71	74	58	65	45	49

There are certain trends and generalizations that should be noted. The results reveal four groups of responses: (a) where the majority of the respondents know the Church's position and personally hold it to be true, (b) where teachers are more likely to know the Church's position but do not hold it personally, (c) where the majority of the respondents do not know the Church's position on a particular issue but hold it as their personal belief, and (d) where teachers have developed no clear consensus of either their knowledge or belief regarding the Church's position on a particular issue.

The good news is that the largest group is the first—teachers who know and believe the Church's position. Most of these responses come from the questions about general Christian and particular Catholic dogma. The not-so-good news comes from two fronts: the first, where teachers know the Church's position but reject it as their personal belief and, worse still, the second, where teachers do not know or believe the Church's position. There should be a good degree of caution used in both areas, however, because it is easy to jump to a conclusion that may not necessarily be the case.

The question arises, Why do so many teachers know the Church's position but not accept it? There may be a host of reasons for this disparity, such as incomplete information, public persuasion, personal experience, or the wording of the statements as presented in this survey. It was not the goal of this study to examine the "why" of the difference between knowledge and belief, just to identify that there are differences between knowledge and belief and what some of the predictors of those differences might be. Regarding the second area, teachers may not know and believe the Church's position simply because they may have never been exposed to it. This could be a call to Church leadership to examine the content and method of preparation for catechists.

It is possible, through a statistical procedure known as regression analysis, to identify "qualities" that can be recognized in teachers who score high in knowledge and belief. Qualities or predictors are those personal background and ritualistic and devotional characteristics by which teachers identified themselves. The pool of potential predictors was of two types: (a) background variables (e.g., personal and demographic characteristics of the teachers, the characteristics of the class they taught, and the certification process that they had undergone to prepare them to teach religion) and (b) frequency variables related to the teachers' participation in 16 devotional and ritual practices.

A regression of knowledge of Church teachings on the teachers' background variables explained nearly 20% of the variance. The predictors that significantly contributed were the teacher's formal religious education, the teacher's age, grade level taught, method of religion teaching certification, school locality, whether or not the teacher was a Catholic by birth or a convert, and the number of years of religion teaching experience.

The regression of personal belief in Church teachings on the teachers' background variables explained approximately 22% of the variance. The predictors were the teacher's age, the teacher's formal religious education, method of religion teaching certification, race of the students, grade level taught, whether or not the teacher was a Catholic by birth or a convert, and the number of years of religion teaching experience.

One way of addressing the questions raised in the discussion of the results in the Appraisal of Church Teaching section of the survey is to examine those teachers who scored higher in the areas of knowledge and belief. The major predictors common to both knowledge of Church teachings and personal belief were formal religious education, age, being a Catholic, grade level taught, number of years of teaching religion, and method of certification. The results indicate that the more formal the religious education a teacher has, the higher the score in both knowledge and belief. The more exposure to religious education, the better a teacher is able to identify and believe Church teachings.

Teachers over 45 years old score higher on both knowledge and belief. There could be several reasons for this. Those over age 45 have more life experience and more of the day-to-day information that comes with such experience. Another reason might be the different experience of the Church that older Catholics have. Many of those over 45 (at the time of the survey) obtained most of their early formal religious education before the changes of the Second Vatican Council took place. Whatever the reason, in general, older teachers seem to have a greater awareness of the religious aspects of a Catholic school.

The method of religion teaching certification was an important factor in determining differences in knowledge and belief scores. The more formal the teacher's course preparation for certification is, the higher the scores in both knowledge and faith. Those with formal college credit courses score markedly higher than teachers in other groups. This finding argues for the implementation of programs to deliver formal religious certification.

The more experience a teacher has in teaching religion, the higher the scores on both knowledge and belief. Perhaps, the more frequently teachers are required to explain the subject matter, the more they understand it and integrate it into to their thinking and life. This finding seems to indicate that if the Church wishes to have teachers who are well-informed and well formed about the faith, it is in its best interest to encourage a policy of faculty retention. It is also an argument for mentoring programs, where more experienced teachers are paired with those less experienced and so foster growth in young teachers.

In addition to these regression results, but not part of them, certification itself makes a difference in knowledge and belief scores. Teachers certified through either a diocese or courses taken in college score higher in both knowledge and belief than those who are not. Those in the process of attending certification programs score higher in both areas than those teaching religion without having undergone any certification process.

Higher scores in both knowledge and personal belief are found among those religion teachers whose classes are composed of more than 90% Catholic students when compared with teachers whose classes have less than 90% Catholic students. This may be due to one of several reasons. First, the schools with less than 90% Catholic students have more non-Catholic teachers, who understandably score lower in knowledge of Church teachings and personal belief. Second, there may be fewer Catholics to be models and fewer opportunities to discuss religious issues. Third, economically poorer schools may have fewer resources or opportunities to obtain or provide updating experiences for the staff. Lastly, there may be more input from non-Catholic influences into the school community. This might well create a form of theological pluralism which, instead of focusing solely on Catholic Church teaching, integrates the teaching of non-Catholic religious faiths.

A surprising finding of this study is that nearly half of the teachers do not encourage vocations to the priesthood and religious life. It was also established that teachers who do encourage vocations score higher in knowledge and belief. The difference in the average personal belief scores is twice that of the difference in the average knowledge scores. There are no data by which comparisons can be made to determine if lay teachers have been strong in their encouragement of vocations in previous years. Do those teachers who encourage vocations have a deeper appreciation of the Church and therefore score higher in knowledge and belief? Does whether or not teachers encourage vocations make a statement about their appreciation of the Church? Are teachers not encouraging vocations because they do not feel this is their role? Is there a shift in the view that lay people have of the religious and priestly life? This issue raises more questions than it answers, but it is one that may offer insight into the knowledge and belief of teachers of religion.

When teachers were asked if they would choose to teach religion even if it were not mandated in their contract, the group that said they would scored significantly higher in both knowledge and personal belief. Perhaps those who would not choose to teach religion are not sufficiently informed about Church teachings. Those who would not choose to teach religion are also less likely to hold as their personal belief what the Church teaches in the areas listed in this survey. Those charged with the hiring of faculty might inquire about an applicant's desire to teach religion and respect the applicant's wishes in this area. Faculty responsibilities should be aligned accordingly.

Besides the specifically personal background variables, ritual and devotional practices were examined for their predictive qualities. The Congregation for Catholic Education (1982) stated that the more completely an educator can give concrete witness to the model of the ideal person that is being presented to the students, the more this ideal will be believed and imitated. Raftery (1985) stated that "witness is the basis of Christian ministry. . . . The teacher is a very visible witness to the school community on a daily basis. This is what makes the responsibility of teacher in the Catholic school so awesome" (p. 33). In this study, the practice dimension variables were used as predictors of the knowledge and belief dimensions.

When the devotional and ritualistic variables were used to predict knowledge of Church teachings, they explained only 10% of the variance. The predictors were receiving Communion, doing non-biblical reading, attending interfaith services, making retreats, meditating, discussing one's faith with others, reciting the rosary, and participating in novenas. The strongest of these predictors were reception of Communion and non-biblical reading.

In a regression of personal belief in Church teachings on devotional and ritualistic predictors, slightly more than 23% of the variance was explained. The predictors were receiving Communion, reciting the rosary, practicing personal prayer, going to confession, participating in Cursillo or other such experiences, meditating, doing non-biblical reading, attending interfaith services, discussing one's faith with others, attending worship services, making retreats, and visiting or phoning friends in need. The strongest predictors here were reception of Communion, recitation of the rosary, personal prayer, and meditation.

These findings support Finney's (1978) contention that activities such as prayer and Bible reading help to legitimate one's religious experiences and beliefs. Devotional activities provide evidence that one's beliefs are "true." From the manner in which the devotional and ritual variables aided in the prediction of knowledge and personal belief, it can be said that the more teachers practice their faith, the more they become in tune with it.

These findings lend support to Buetow's (1988) observation that the way to increase the faith dimension of the teacher is to provide more opportunities for such activities as prayer, discussion, faith sharing, and retreats.

There are four major findings of this study and one important non-conclusion. The findings are the following:

1. A dramatic shift has taken place over the last 30 years in the composition of religion teachers at the elementary school level in Catholic schools. Where they were once predominantly members of religious congregations, today most teachers are members of the laity. These lay teachers bring with them a host of varied and valuable experiences that shape their understanding of the Church and its teachings.

2. In general, lay teachers of religion are well-informed (i.e., knowledgeable) in some areas of religious knowledge but poorly informed in others.

3. In general, lay teachers of religion believe as the Church believes in certain religious issues, but they do not personally accept the Church's beliefs in certain other religious issues.

4. If religious knowledge and religious belief are important factors in the hiring of lay teachers, then the most important characteristics to look for in teachers are age (the older the better), the number of years of religious education (again, the more the better), and the method of teaching certification (the more formal the education, the better).

The non-conclusion of this study is nearly as important. It cannot be said what makes a "good" teacher of religion. As anyone in administration can tell, it takes a lot more than knowledge of the subject matter to be a good teacher. This study did not examine the effectiveness of teachers in their ability to transmit or hand on the faith to their students. One of the questions that is raised by the implications of the present research, however, is: How can someone effectively teach something they do not believe? When students raise a question sincerely wanting to know why they should believe a teaching of the Church, the effective teacher is able to explain an answer from both the cognitive and affective dimensions. In written responses that accompanied this survey, many teachers say that they taught the Church's position even though they do not themselves believe that position. In some areas this was not the case because of the teacher's inability to correctly identify the Church's position. In several other instances, teachers identify an errant position as the Church's teaching, and yet they personally believe what the correct Church teaching is. Even more serious is the group of issues in which teachers cannot identify the Church's teaching in either the knowledge or belief category. One must ask, What is being taught here?

Some of the results here are quite positive, but others are quite disturbing. Moving beyond the statistical data, some policy recommendations need to be made and some pertinent questions asked for the future of Catholic education:

1. There is a need for guidelines in the teaching of religion. The focus of these guidelines should be on the content of what is taught at each level of education and on what the appropriate response is. These guidelines should address cognitive content of courses but must also provide help with methodological issues that affect religious education in particular. Too often, the textbook of a lower grade level is similar to that of a higher grade level. Religion is a spiral curriculum that needs to be nuanced at the various levels. Teachers do not know what to teach at the various levels because this has not been clearly defined as is the case in other subject matters, such as mathematics, science, and social studies. These guidelines would help alleviate this problem and lend a much-needed degree of professionalism to the teaching of religion.

2. Where possible, a diocese should take advantage of local colleges and universities and make arrangements with them for certification classes for catechists. No doubt, arrangements for tuition and credit are problems that will arise, but it is in the best interest of both the diocese and the colleges to accommodate one another. An important finding of the present research is that certification by itself is not the answer; it is the method of certification that is most important to knowledge of and belief in the teachings of the Church.

3. Schools are encouraged to make faculty retention a goal if knowledge of and belief in Church teachings and sense of community among the faculty are desired objectives. The longer one teaches, the more prone one is to know and believe the teachings of the Church. It is in the best interest of Catholic elementary schools to have established faculties where the teaching

of religion is done by competent and experienced teachers. This policy of retention can be encouraged by offering better pay, improving working conditions, fostering the sense of commitment that exists in teachers, or appealing to their sense of ministry. As Buetow (1988) stated in referring to the *General Catechetical Directory:* "The selection of religion teachers must ... receive the greatest of care. Only those who are distinguished by ability, learning and spiritual life are to be chosen for so important a task" (p. 256).

4. Priests and those charged with leading congregations of worshipers should take greater advantage of the opportunity presented to them in weekly sermons to be educators of the Christian faith. The written responses of teachers surveyed indicate that they want to hear more from their parish leaders about the cognitive content of their faith. Homilists and preachers need to be more attentive to their role as educators and provide not only spiritual reflections but also substantive material that helps explain the faith to their congregations. One cannot assume that everybody knows their faith. Education and discussion are great supplements in the struggle to live a good moral life.

5. More research needs to be done to explore the disparity that exists between catechists' knowledge and belief. Why are people not accepting the teachings of the Church, most especially on moral issues? It can be conjectured that most people receive their information about Church teachings from the secular press, and this is not good. There is an inherent bias in the secular press that looks for the sensational and the divisive. The Church needs to do a better job of communicating its teachings and explaining the reasons behind those teachings. At their roots, these teachings are not capricious statements; rather, they are instructions that are for the betterment of the human race.

6. A change in attitude must take place on the part of those who provide resources for those who teach. It must be realized that most of today's teachers of religion are married and have children living at home with them. The time these teachers have to dedicate to the preparation of religion classes needs to be optimized. Resource books and information need to be made available that contain in one place the necessary information that will help teachers be more effective; for example, articles on how children learn religion and how skills can be taught. Easy-to-read material needs to be provided also for new teachers of religion, since there is such a high turnover rate in Catholic schools. Schools need to compensate for the lack of experience and of familiarity with the material that these new teachers have.

7. In a study done in the mid-1960s, two researchers, Stark and Glock, studied various religious faiths. Among the many results was one that showed that Catholics felt they knew the most about their faith when, in fact, they were the worst informed of any religious groups. (In fact, members of the Jewish faith knew more information about the New Testament than did

Catholics!) This finding is a clarion call that we cannot be satisfied with the feeling we derive from our opinions. As a church, we need to realize the importance of educational experiences in the faith life of people.

The present research and the research of others, most especially Andrew Greeley's work, confirm that Catholic schools do work and do make a difference as regards the knowledge and beliefs of students; we have to acknowledge that and be proud of it. Ignorance, in its broadest sense, is going to change our Catholic faith, and this will not be for the better. Catholic schools are a financial investment that is well worth the cost because ignorance of faith is too high a price to pay. We as a church— clergy and laity—must be willing to make the sacrifices of time and money that are needed to keep these institutions of religious formation alive. They are the places where we teach the three *R*'s of Catholic education: Respect, Responsibility, and Religion. If for no other reason, we must keep Catholic education a viable alternative for the sake of our children and their relationship with God.

Appendix

THE CATHOLIC UNIVERSITY OF AMERICA

Department of Education
Washington, D.C. 20064
202-319-5800

Dear Teacher of Religion,

Thank you for taking the time to participate in this survey. I myself am a teacher and realize that you have many obligations and demands on your time. I sincerely appreciate this effort. This is the first time that a national survey of elementary school teachers of religion has ever been undertaken. There are about 4000 teachers participating. Your involvement is important because the results of this survey will be made available to those who make policy in the area of religious education and so your voice should be heard.

Some guidelines to help you.
1. The survey should take between 20 and 25 minutes to complete.
2. Please be sure to answer <u>every</u> question.
3. Every question can receive <u>only one answer</u>. In some cases you might like to choose two, but please, only one answer per question.
4. In several cases you may not find an answer that exactly expresses your opinion or understanding of a certain issue. In that case, choose the answer that <u>comes closest</u>.
5. You can only use a no. 2 pencil to fill in the responses. You may use the pencil provided with this survey and keep it after you have finished.
6. Place the completed survey in the pre-stamped, pre-addressed envelope. This will ensure your confidentiality and anonymity. Please mail it as soon as you can. The numbers on the survey form are for control purposes only and will not be used to identify any particular survey.

Again, thank you for taking the time to respond to this survey.

Appreciatively,

Fr. Paul W. Galetto, OSA

Fr. Paul W. Galetto, OSA

Survey of Catholic Elementary School Teachers of Religion

Please answer the following questions by choosing the response that best fits your particular situation.

DO NOT MARK HERE ➡ ○○○○○○○○○○

§ SCANTRON FORM NO. 25918-FPG
© SCANTRON CORPORATION 1994 P4 1294-C E3510- 5 4 3 2 1
ALL RIGHTS RESERVED.

INSTRUCTIONS: Please use a No. 2 pencil and make sure you fill in the box completely and darkly, erasing any mistakes and stray marks. Do not use ink or ball point pen.

✦ CORRECT ○
✦ INCORRECT ⦸ ⊗ ⊘

I. General Information.

A. Teacher Information

1. Please indicate your gender:
   ○ Female   ○ Male

2. Which of the following describes your racial/ethnic background?
   ○ American Indian/Alaskan   ○ Hispanic
   ○ Asian/Pacific Islander   ○ White or other
   ○ Black, non-Hispanic

3. How old are you?
   ○ Under 25   ○ 45 - 54
   ○ 25 - 34   ○ 55 or older
   ○ 35 - 44

4. Which of the following best applies to you?
   ○ I was born a Catholic   ○ I am not a Catholic
   ○ I am a convert to Catholicism

5. What is your highest educational level?
   ○ High School
   ○ College
   ○ College with additional graduate credits
   ○ Master's degree
   ○ Master's degree with additional graduate credits
   ○ Doctorate

6. Do you have any graduate credits in religion or theology?
   ○ None   ○ 13-24
   ○ 1-12   ○ More than 24

7. How many years of formal religious education (school-based or parish-based courses or programs) have you had before the age of 23?
   ○ None   ○ Between 9 and 12
   ○ Between 1 and 4   ○ More than 12 years
   ○ Between 5 and 8

8. How many years of your formal education (in question #7 above) were in

Catholic Elementary School?	Catholic High School?	Catholic College?
○ None	○ None	○ None
○ 1 - 3	○ 1	○ 1
○ 4 - 6	○ 2	○ 2
○ 7 - 9	○ 3	○ 3
	○ 4 or more	○ 4 or more

9. Which of the following best describes you?
   ○ I have never attempted to become a priest, religious brother or religious sister.
   ○ I experienced initial formation as a religious/priest but made no commitment (vows).
   ○ I made simple profession in a religious group/received minor orders.
   ○ I made solemn (or perpetual) vows in a religious group/was ordained (deacon or priest).

10. Which statement best describes your present situation?
    ○ Religious sister, religious brother or priest
    ○ Single
    ○ Married
    ○ Widowed
    ○ Separated/Divorced (but not remarried)
    ○ Remarried after a divorce and annulment
    ○ Remarried after a divorce without an annulment

11. Do you have children living at home with you?
    ○ Yes   ○ No

12. What grade level do you primarily teach?
    ○ All different grade levels   ○ 4th to 6th
    ○ Pre-school - Kindergarten   ○ 7th to 8th
    ○ 1st to 3rd

B. Teaching Situation

13. Which best describes the locality where you teach?
    ○ Inner-City   ○ Suburban
    ○ City   ○ Rural

14. What percentage of your religion students are Catholic?
    ○ 90 - 100%   ○ 40 - 49 %
    ○ 60 - 89 %   ○ 30 - 39%
    ○ 50 - 59%   ○ Less than 30%

15. Do you teach religion
    ○ in Catholic schools only
    ○ in both Catholic schools and Religious Education Programs
    ○ in Religious Education Programs only

16. How many years have you taught in a Catholic school?
    ○ 0 - 5   ○ 16 - 20
    ○ 6 - 10   ○ Over 20 years
    ○ 11 - 15

6223

MAKE NO MARKS IN THIS AREA

17. How many years have you taught religion in a Catholic school?
    - ○ 0 - 5
    - ○ 6 - 10
    - ○ 11 - 15
    - ○ 16 - 20
    - ○ Over 20 years

18. Which best describes your situation?
    - ○ I am certified to teach religion by the (arch)diocese.
    - ○ I am certified to teach religion because of college courses I have taken.
    - ○ I am teaching religion while I am attending certification courses.
    - ○ I am teaching religion without having undergone a certification program.

19. Which of the following best describes your current status as a religion teacher?
    - ○ I have never taken any informal or formal courses in order to prepare me to teach religion.
    - ○ The majority of my preparation for teaching religion has been informal instruction (e.g., local in-service programs, watching videos).
    - ○ The majority of my preparation for teaching religion has been formal non-college credit course(s) (e.g., program sponsored by the diocese).
    - ○ The majority of my preparation for teaching religion has been formal college credit courses.

20. The permanent certification process for teaching religion in my diocese requires:
    - ○ 1 to 2 courses (3 to 6 credits/hours)
    - ○ 3 to 4 courses (9 to 12 credits/hours)
    - ○ 5 to 6 courses (15 to 18 credits/hours)
    - ○ More than 6 courses (more than 18 credits/hours)
    - ○ There is no certification process in my diocese.
    - ○ I am not sure/aware of the requirements for certification.

21. During this current school year, how many hours of updating will you receive with respect to being a teacher of religion?
    - ○ None
    - ○ 1 - 8 hours (one day)
    - ○ 9 - 16 hours (two days)
    - ○ 17 - 24 hours (three days)
    - ○ More than 24 hours

22. Which statement best describes the majority of the religion students you teach?
    - ○ Poor
    - ○ Lower middle class
    - ○ Middle middle class
    - ○ Upper middle class
    - ○ Wealthy

23. What is the ethnic background of the majority of the religion students you teach?
    - ○ American Indian/Alaskan
    - ○ Asian/Pacific Islander
    - ○ Black, non-Hispanic
    - ○ Hispanic
    - ○ White or other
    - ○ No clear majority

C. Teacher Opinion

Using the scale indicated, how do you feel about the following issues:

	Very Satisfied 4	Satisfied 3	Unsatisfied 2	Very Unsatisfied 1	Not Applicable 0
24. Your qualifications to teach in general.	○	○	○	○	○
25. Your enjoyment of teaching overall.	○	○	○	○	○
26. Your qualifications to teach religion.	○	○	○	○	○
27. Your enjoyment of teaching religion.	○	○	○	○	○
28. The difference you have made in the faith life of your students.	○	○	○	○	○
29. Your sense of accomplishment in teaching religion.	○	○	○	○	○
30. Your students' achievement in overall learning.	○	○	○	○	○
31. Your sense of accomplishment in teaching in general.	○	○	○	○	○
32. Your students' achievement in learning religion.	○	○	○	○	○
33. Your knowledge of Church teachings.	○	○	○	○	○
34. Your personal devotional religious life.	○	○	○	○	○
35. The sense of a faith community in your school.	○	○	○	○	○

Using the scale indicated, how do you feel about the following issues:

	Strongly Agree 4	Agree 3	Disagree 2	Strongly Disagree 1
36. When it comes right down to it, a teacher really can't do much to help a student's <u>overall learning</u> because most of a student's motivation and performance depends on his or her home environment.	○	○	○	○
37. If I really try hard when I'm <u>teaching in general</u>, I can get through to even the most difficult or unmotivated students.	○	○	○	○
38. When it comes right down to it, a teacher really can't do much to help a student's <u>knowledge</u> because most of a student's motivation and performance depends on his or her home environment.	○	○	○	○

111

Using the scale indicated, how do you feel about the following issues:

		Strongly Agree 4	Agree 3	Disagree 2	Strongly Disagree 1
39.	If I really try hard when I'm <u>teaching about the Catholic faith</u>, I can get through to even the most difficult or unmotivated students.	○	○	○	○
40.	When it comes right down to it, a teacher really can't do much to help a student's <u>practice of religion</u> because most of a student's motivation and performance depends on his or her home environment.	○	○	○	○
41.	If I really try hard, I can help a student improve his or her <u>practice of religion</u>, even with the most difficult or unmotivated students.	○	○	○	○
42.	I actively encourage vocations to the priesthood and religious life.	○	○	○	○
43.	The demands made on me as a teacher of religion conflict with my home responsibilities.	○	○	○	○

44.	Does your teaching position require you to teach religion?	○ Yes		○ No
45.	If your teaching agreement did not require you to teach religion, would you still choose to do so?	○ Yes		○ No

46. Answer YES or NO to the following. In the following instances the word "regularly" is used. Some things are "regular" if they occur every six months (e.g., visiting the dentist), some if they occur every day (e.g., eating breakfast). Please use your personal discretion to determine what regular means here:

a.	Does the faculty regularly pray together?	○ Yes	○ No
b.	Are faculty retreats regularly made available to you?	○ Yes	○ No
c.	Is there religious updating regularly provided to religion teachers?	○ Yes	○ No
d.	Are opportunities for Eucharist regularly available to you as a faculty member?	○ Yes	○ No
e.	Are opportunities for Reconciliation regularly available to you as a faculty member?	○ Yes	○ No

47. Please describe your salary:
   ○ More than adequate
   ○ Adequate
   ○ Inadequate
   ○ More than inadequate
   ○ I volunteer and therefore do not receive a salary.

48. Which statement best describes your parish financial contribution pattern:
   ○ My teaching in a Catholic school does not affect the amount I contribute in my parish offering.
   ○ Since I teach in a Catholic school, I give less than I would otherwise in my parish offering.
   ○ Since I teach in a Catholic school, I do not feel I need to make an additional contribution through my parish offering.

6223

MAKE NO MARKS IN THIS AREA

II. Appraisal of Church Teaching

In the following section, a selection of statements is given with regard to certain theological and moral issues. For each set you are asked to identify first, the Church's position as you understand it and second, the statement that comes closest to identifying your personal position on the issue.

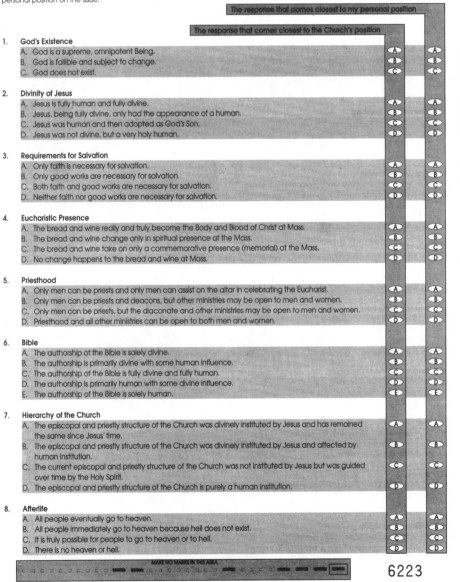

The response that comes closest to my personal position

The response that comes closest to the Church's position

1. **God's Existence**
   A. God is a supreme, omnipotent Being.
   B. God is fallible and subject to change.
   C. God does not exist.

2. **Divinity of Jesus**
   A. Jesus is fully human and fully divine.
   B. Jesus, being fully divine, only had the appearance of a human.
   C. Jesus was human and then adopted as God's Son.
   D. Jesus was not divine, but a very holy human.

3. **Requirements for Salvation**
   A. Only faith is necessary for salvation.
   B. Only good works are necessary for salvation.
   C. Both faith and good works are necessary for salvation.
   D. Neither faith nor good works are necessary for salvation.

4. **Eucharistic Presence**
   A. The bread and wine really and truly become the Body and Blood of Christ at Mass.
   B. The bread and wine change only in spiritual presence at the Mass.
   C. The bread and wine take on only a commemorative presence (memorial) at the Mass.
   D. No change happens to the bread and wine at Mass.

5. **Priesthood**
   A. Only men can be priests and only men can assist on the altar in celebrating the Eucharist.
   B. Only men can be priests and deacons, but other ministries may be open to men and women.
   C. Only men can be priests, but the diaconate and other ministries may be open to men and women.
   D. Priesthood and all other ministries can be open to both men and women.

6. **Bible**
   A. The authorship of the Bible is solely divine.
   B. The authorship is primarily divine with some human influence.
   C. The authorship of the Bible is fully divine and fully human.
   D. The authorship is primarily human with some divine influence.
   E. The authorship of the Bible is solely human.

7. **Hierarchy of the Church**
   A. The episcopal and priestly structure of the Church was divinely instituted by Jesus and has remained the same since Jesus' time.
   B. The episcopal and priestly structure of the Church was divinely instituted by Jesus and affected by human institution.
   C. The current episcopal and priestly structure of the Church was not instituted by Jesus but was guided over time by the Holy Spirit.
   D. The episcopal and priestly structure of the Church is purely a human institution.

8. **Afterlife**
   A. All people eventually go to heaven.
   B. All people immediately go to heaven because hell does not exist.
   C. It is truly possible for people to go to heaven or to hell.
   D. There is no heaven or hell.

MAKE NO MARKS IN THIS AREA.

6223

9. **Infallibility of the Pope**
   A. The Pope is infallible in all matters.
   B. The Pope is infallible in all matters regarding the Church only.
   C. The Pope is infallible in matters of faith and morals only.
   D. The Pope can never claim infallibility.

10. **Elective Abortion**
    A. Direct elective abortion is wrong in all situations.
    B. Direct elective abortion is wrong except to save the life of the mother.
    C. Direct elective abortion is wrong except to save the life of the mother and in cases of rape or incest.
    D. Direct elective abortion is an individual's right under most circumstances.

11. **Church Moral Teaching**
    A. People must accept everything the Church teaches about morals at all times.
    B. People must accept everything the Church teaches about morals except in particular circumstances.
    C. Church teaching is an essential component in a moral decision.
    D. Church teaching is merely an opinion on a particular issue.

12. **Artificial Birth Control**
    A. Artificial birth control is never appropriate in marriage.
    B. Artificial birth control is appropriate only when the wife's health is endangered.
    C. Artificial birth control is permissible in marriage as long as the couple does have the intention to have children at some point in time.
    D. Artificial birth control is not morally wrong.

13. **Role of Mary**
    A. Mary's role in our salvation is as important as the role of Jesus.
    B. Mary's role in salvation is unique, distinct from that of Jesus and the saints.
    C. Mary's role in salvation is the same as other saints.
    D. Mary has no special role in salvation.

14. **Existence of the Devil**
    A. The devil is not as powerful as God.
    B. The devil is as powerful as God.
    C. The devil is more powerful than God.
    D. The devil does not exist.

15. **Resurrection**
    A. Jesus rose bodily from the dead.
    B. Jesus rose only in spirit from the dead.
    C. Jesus did not rise from the dead.

16. **Predestination**
    A. God predestines everyone to salvation.
    B. God predestines some to salvation and some to damnation.
    C. God predestines no one.

17. **Salvation**
    A. Only those who believe in Jesus can attain heaven.
    B. Only those who believe in God can attain heaven.
    C. Anyone can attain heaven.

18. **Suffering in the World**
    A. God causes us to suffer for our benefit.
    B. God does not intend suffering, but allows it.
    C. God is powerless to prevent suffering.

The response that comes closest to my personal position

The response that comes closest to the Church's position

19. **Marriage**
   A. Under no circumstances, except for the death of a spouse, may a Catholic enter into a second marriage.
   B. Under no circumstances, except for the death of a spouse or where an annulment or dissolution has been granted, may a Catholic enter into a second marriage.
   C. A Catholic may enter into a second marriage if either of the spouses in the first marriage commits adultery.
   D. A Catholic may enter into a second marriage if either of the spouses in the first marriage commits adultery or if there is physical or emotional abuse.
   E. Incompatibility in the first marriage would allow a Catholic to enter into a second marriage.

20. **Euthanasia**
   A. Dying people should always be provided needed nutrition.
   B. Dying people should always be provided needed nutrition except when to do so would involve an extraordinary means of preserving life.
   C. Dying people should always be provided needed nutrition except for those in great pain.
   D. Dying people should always be provided needed nutrition except for those whose quality of life has been lessened.

21. **Discrimination**
   A. All people deserve equal opportunity.
   B. Some people deserve equal opportunity while others must earn it.
   C. All people must earn equal opportunity.
   D. Not all people deserve equal opportunity.

22. **Homosexuality**
   A. Homosexuals by orientation are to be treated as outside the Church.
   B. Homosexuals by orientation are to be treated as sinners in need of forgiveness and are not full members of the Church.
   C. Homosexuals by orientation can be full members of the Church.

23. **Premarital Sex**
   A. Premarital sex is always morally wrong.
   B. Premarital sex is permissible when the couple is engaged.
   C. Premarital sex is permissible after a couple has been dating for a period of time.
   D. Premarital sex is not morally wrong.

24. **Reception of Communion**
   A. Only Catholics can receive the Eucharist at a Catholic service.
   B. Only Catholics and those who believe in real presence may receive the Eucharist at a Catholic service.
   C. Any Christian may receive the Eucharist at a Catholic service.
   D. Anyone who wishes may receive the Eucharist at a Catholic service.

25. **Sacrament of Penance**
   A. In order for any sin to be forgiven, a Catholic must receive the Sacrament of Penance.
   B. A Catholic must receive the Sacrament of Penance once a year even if he or she has committed only minor (venial) sins.
   C. It is necessary to receive the Sacrament of Penance only if a Catholic has committed mortal sins.
   D. There is no need for a Sacrament of Penance because God knows our sins and only God can forgive them.
   E. There is no need for the Sacrament of Penance because sins are between the individual person and the one offended.

MAKE NO MARKS IN THIS AREA

6223

III. Religious Practice:

Please choose that response which best describes your level of participation in the religious practice that is mentioned:

		Every Day	Several Times per Week	Once a Week	2-3 Times per Month	Once a Month	Several Times a Year	About Once a Year	Never
1.	Attend Worship Services (e.g., Mass/Eucharist)	○	○	○	○	○	○	○	○
2.	Recite the Rosary	○	○	○	○	○	○	○	○
3.	Participate in a Novena	○	○	○	○	○	○	○	○
4.	Read the Bible	○	○	○	○	○	○	○	○
5.	Do non-Biblical spiritual reading	○	○	○	○	○	○	○	○
6.	Personal Prayer	○	○	○	○	○	○	○	○
7.	Private Meditation (quiet time)	○	○	○	○	○	○	○	○
8.	Go to confession (Reconciliation)	○	○	○	○	○	○	○	○
9.	Say grace before meals	○	○	○	○	○	○	○	○
10.	Discuss your religious beliefs with others	○	○	○	○	○	○	○	○
11.	Visit or phone a friend or neighbor in need	○	○	○	○	○	○	○	○
12.	Take part in a parish adult education program (Bible study, etc.)	○	○	○	○	○	○	○	○
13.	Receive Communion	○	○	○	○	○	○	○	○

14. How often do you make a personal retreat?
○ more than once a year ○ yearly ○ every several years ○ rarely ○ never

15. How often do you take part in an inter-faith service?
○ more than once a year ○ yearly ○ every several years ○ rarely ○ never

16. How often do you participate in renewal experiences (such as: Marriage Encounter, Cursillo, RENEW, etc.)?
○ more than once a year ○ yearly ○ every several years ○ rarely ○ never

IV. Developing the Christian Lifestyle in Students:

Please choose the statement that best articulates your position. **Choose only one** statement per question.

1. It is most important that my religion students
   ○ understand the teachings of the Church.
   ○ believe the teachings of the Church.
   ○ act on the teachings of the Church.

2. For me, the most important objective in the religion courses I teach is that my students
   ○ respond to life's situations in Christian ways.
   ○ are able to express confidence in their beliefs.
   ○ understand why they believe.

3. The greatest goal my students can achieve is
   ○ knowledge of the faith.
   ○ the ability to live in Christian ways.
   ○ trust in God.

4. I consider myself to have been most successful if my students
   ○ become trusting individuals.
   ○ are convicted about the beliefs of their faith.
   ○ become more involved in helping others.

5. In my religion class preparations, I feel it is most important
   ○ to make sure that Church teachings are presented accurately.
   ○ to suggest opportunities and ways that one's faith can be lived.
   ○ to develop a sense of trust in God.

6. I am doing my best job teaching religion
   ○ when I emphasize involvement in the community.
   ○ when I clearly identify what makes someone a Christian.
   ○ if I can develop within my students a trusting reliance in God.

7. Faith, as I present it, is best associated with
   ○ believing.
   ○ trusting.
   ○ doing.

8. I judge my students to be most successful when their faith is exhibited as
   ○ knowledge.
   ○ practice.
   ○ action.

9. If and when I use the Bible in my classes, it is primarily
   ○ to let students read about their faith from a first-hand source.
   ○ to allow students to become familiar with the mystery of God's actions.
   ○ to let students experience stories of how faith causes people to act.

10. In teaching religion, I find the lesson to be most effective for the students when I
    ○ challenge them to have confidence in their faith.
    ○ give examples of how people live out their faith.
    ○ mention or discuss important issues of the day.

References
and Resources

Ashton, P., et al. (1983). *A study of teachers' sense of efficacy* (Final report, executive summary). Washington, DC: National Institute of Education. (ERIC Document Reproduction Service No. ED 231 833)

Augustine, St., of Hippo. (1978). *The first catechetical instruction* (The Rev. J. P. Christopher, Trans.). Ramsey, NJ: Paulist Press.

Bandura, A. (1982). Self-efficacy mechanism in human agency. *American Psychologist, 37*(2), 122-147.

Baum, W. (1989). Christian education of the young. *Origins, 18,* 708-711.

Benson, P., & Guerra, M. (1985). *Sharing the faith: The beliefs and values of Catholic high school teachers.* Washington, DC: National Catholic Educational Association.

Bernardin, J. L. (1974). Bishops, theologians, religion teachers: Their roles. *Origins, 3,* 101-104.

Bernardin, J. L. (1989). Catholic schools: Opportunities and challenges. *Chicago Studies, 28*(3), 264-276.

Bitter, G. (1984). What faith shall we hand on? Can it be reduced to kerygmatic essentials? *Concilium, 174,* pp. 39-44.

Braxton, E. (1986). The catechist's ministry: An intimate dialogue of the soul. *Origins, 16,* 489-496.

Brigham, F. H., Jr. (1990). *United States Catholic elementary and secondary schools 1989-1990: Annual statistical report on schools, enrollment and staffing.* Washington, DC: National Catholic Educational Association.

Brigham, F. H., Jr. (1994). *United States Catholic elementary and secondary schools 1993-1994: Annual statistical report on schools, enrollment and staffing.* Washington, DC: National Catholic Educational Association.

Bryk, A., Lee, V., & Holland, P. (1993). *Catholic schools and the common good*. Cambridge, MA: Harvard University Press.

Buetow, H. (1988). *The Catholic school: Its roots, identity, and future*. New York: Crossoad.

Campbell, T., & Fukuyama, Y. (1970). *The fragmented layman*. Philadelphia: Pilgrim Press.

Ciriello, M. (1987). *Teachers in Catholic schools: A study of commitment* [CD-ROM]. Abstract from: ProQuest File: Dissertation Abstracts Item: 8713567.

Code of Canon Law (Latin-English edition). (1983). Washington, DC: Canon Law Society of America.

Congregation for Catholic Education. (1977). The Catholic school. *The Pope Speaks, 22,* 332-357.

Congregation for Catholic Education. (1982). Lay teachers: Witnesses to faith. *The Pope Speaks, 28,* 45-73.

Congregation for Catholic Education. (1988). *The religious dimension of education in a Catholic school* (Publication No. 231-4). Washington, DC: United States Catholic Conference.

Congregation for the Clergy. (1971). The general catechetical directory. In B. L. Marthaler (Ed.), *Catechetics in context* (pp. 2-280). Huntington, IN: Our Sunday Visitor, Inc.

Congregation for the Doctrine of the Faith. (1975). Declaration on certain questions concerning sexual ethics. *The Pope Speaks, 21,* 60-73.

Congregation for the Doctrine of the Faith. (1980). Declaration on euthanasia. *Origins, 10,* 154-157.

Congregation for the Doctrine of the Faith. (1986). Declaration on homosexuals. *The Pope Speaks, 32,* 62-68.

Convey, J. J. (1992). *Catholic schools make a difference: Twenty-five years of research*. Washington, DC: National Catholic Educational Association.

DeJong, G. F., Faulkner, J. E., & Warland, R. H. (1976). Dimensions of religiosity reconsidered: Evidence from a cross-cultural study. *Social Forces, 54*, 866-889.

Denzinger, H., & Schönmetzer, A. (1975). *Enchiridion symbolorum definitionum et declarationum.* In J. Neuner & J. DuPuis (Eds.), *The Christian faith.* Westminster, MD: Christian Classics, Inc.

Fichter, J. H. (1969). Sociological measurement of religiosity. *Review of Religious Research, 10*, 169-177.

Fichter, J. H. (1988). *A sociologist looks at religion.* Wilmington, DE: Michael Glazier, Inc.

Finney, J. (1978). A theory of religious commitment. *Sociological Analysis, 39*, 19-35.

Fowler, J. (1984). A gradual introduction into the faith. *Concilium, 174*, pp. 39-44.

Fowler, J. (1991). Stages in faith consciousness. In F. K. Oser & W. G. Scarlett (Eds.), *Religious development in childhood and adolescence* (New Directions for Child Development No. 52, pp. 27-45). San Francisco: Jossey-Bass.

Fukuyama, Y. (1961). The major dimensions of church membership. *Review of Religious Research, 2*, 154-161.

Gibbs, J. O., & Crader, K. W. (1970). A criticism of two recent attempts to scale Glock and Stark's dimensions of religiosity. *Sociological Analysis, 31*, 107-114.

Glock, C. Y. (1962). On the study of religious commitment. *Religious Education, Research Supplement, 42*, 98-110.

Gorsuch, R. L. (1984). Measurement: The boon and bane of investigating religion. *American Psychologist, 39*, 228-236.

Greeley, A. (1989). My research on Catholic schools. *Chicago Studies, 28*(3), 245-263.

Greeley, A., & Rossi, P. (1966). *The education of Catholic Americans.* Chicago: Aldine Publishing Company.

Greenwood, G. E., Olejnik, S. F., & Parkay, F. W. (1990). Relationships between four teacher efficacy belief patterns and selected teacher characteristics. *Journal of Research and Development in Education, 23,* 102-106.

Groome, T. (1980). *Christian religious education: Sharing our story and vision.* San Francisco: Harper and Row.

Guerra, M. (1991). *Lighting new fires: Catholic schooling in America 25 years after Vatican II.* Washington, DC: National Catholic Educational Association.

Hickey, J. (1993). "Proclaiming the Gospel with joy: Evangelization in the schools" [Pastoral letter]. Washington, DC.

Hoge, D. R., Heffernan, E., Hemrick, E. F., Nelsen, H. M., O'Connor, J. P., Philibert, P. J., & Thompson, A. D. (1982). Desired outcomes of religious education and youth ministry in six denominations. *Review of Religious Research, 23,* 230-254.

Hume, G. B. (1990). *Catholic education: Transforming the world—A pastor's viewpoint.* Washington, DC: National Catholic Educational Association.

International Council for Catechesis. (1990). *Adult catechesis in the Christian community: Some principles and guidelines.* Vatican City: Libreria Editrice Vaticana.

John Paul II. (1979). *Catechesi tradendae* (Publication No. 654-9). Washington, DC: United States Catholic Conference.

John Paul II. (1984a). Salvifici doloris. *Origins, 13,* 608-624.

John Paul II. (1984b). Support asked for Catholic schools. *Origins, 14,* 225-228.

John Paul II. (1992). Essential criterion: Fidelity to Church teaching. *The pope speaks to the American Church: John Paul II's homilies, speeches, and letters to Catholics in the United States.* San Francisco: Harper Collins Publishers.

John Paul II. (1993). Fidei depositum. *Origins, 22*, 525-529.

Johnston, M. (1995). *The new Catholic catechism—A guide.* Washington, DC: National Catholic Educational Association.

Kelly, F. D. (Ed.). (1991). *What makes a school Catholic?* Washington, DC: National Catholic Educational Association.

Kelly, F. D., Benson, P., & Donahue, M. (1986). *Toward effective parish religious education for children and young people.* Washington, DC: National Catholic Educational Association.

Kohlberg, L. (1984). *Essays on moral development. Vol. 2: The psychology of moral development.* San Francisco: Harper and Row.

Kushner, R., & Helbling, M. (1995). *The people who work there: The report of the Catholic elementary school teacher survey.* Washington, DC: National Catholic Educational Association.

Lee, V. E., Dedrick, R. F., & Smith, J. B. (1991). The effect of the social organization of schools on teachers' efficacy and satisfaction. *Sociology of Education, 64*, 190-208.

Lehman, E. C., & Shriver, D. W. (1968). Academic discipline as predictive of faculty religiosity. *Social Forces, 47*, 171-182.

Malone, J. (1989). The religious dimension of Catholic education. *Chicago Studies, 28*(3), 264-276.

Manno, B. V. (1984, October 27). Lay involvement in Catholic schools. *America*, 246-247.

Maranell, G. M. (1974). *Responses to religion: Studies in the social psychology of religious belief.* Lawrence, KS: University Press of Kansas.

Marthaler, B. L. (1973). *Catechetics in context.* Huntington, IN: Our Sunday Visitor, Inc.

Marthaler, B. L. (1983). The modern catechetical movement in Roman Catholicism: Issues and personalities. In M. Warren (Ed.), *Source book for modern catechetics* (pp. 275-289). Winona, MN: St. Mary's Press.

Myers, J. (1993). To reach full knowledge of the truth: Pastoral on catechesis. *Origins, 22,* 593-601.

O'Brien, J. S. (1988). *An urgent task: What bishops and priests say about religious education programs.* Washington, DC: National Catholic Educational Association.

The Official Catholic Directory. (1983). New Providence, NJ: P. J. Kenedy and Sons.

The Official Catholic Directory. (1986). New Providence, NJ: P. J. Kenedy and Sons.

The Official Catholic Directory. (1989). New Providence, NJ: P. J. Kenedy and Sons.

The Official Catholic Directory. (1993). New Providence, NJ: P. J. Kenedy and Sons.

Paul VI. (1968). Humanae vitae. *The Pope Speaks, 13,* 329-346.

Paul VI. (1974). Declaration on abortion. *The Pope Speaks, 19,* 250-262.

Philbert, P., & Hoge, D. (1982). Teachers, pedagogy and the process of religious education. *Review of Religious Research, 23,* 264-285.

Pilarczyk, D. (1977). When disputes arise. *Origins, 7,* 264-267.

Pius XI. (1930). *Casti connubii.* New York: Sheed and Ward.

Pius XII. (1943). *Divino afflante spiritu.* Washington, DC: National Catholic Welfare Conference.

Princeton Religion Research Center. (in press). *Religion in America: 1995 supplement.* Princeton, NJ: Author.

Raftery, F. (1985). *The teacher in the Catholic school.* Washington, DC: National Catholic Educational Association.

Reese, T. J. (1990). *The universal catechism reader.* San Francisco: Harper Collins Publishers.

Roof, W. C. (1979). Concepts and indicators of religious commitment: A critical review. In R. Wuthnow (Ed.), *The religious dimension: New directions in quantitative research* (pp. 17-45). New York: Academic Press.

Second Vatican Council. (1965a). Declaration on Christian education. Vatican City: Libreria Editrice Vaticana.

Second Vatican Council. (1965b). Declaration on the relation of the Church to non-Christian religions. Vatican City: Libreria Editrice Vaticana.

Second Vatican Council. (1965c). Dogmatic constitution on divine revelation. Vatican City: Libreria Editrice Vaticana.

Second Vatican Council. (1965d). Pastoral constitution on the Church in the modern world. Vatican City: Libreria Editrice Vaticana.

Second Vatican Council. (1964a). Decree on ecumenism. Vatican City: Libreria Editrice Vaticana.

Second Vatican Council. (1964b). Dogmatic constitution on the Church. Vatican City: Libreria Editrice Vaticana.

Stark, R., & Glock, C. Y. (1968). *American piety: The nature of religious commitment*. Berkeley: University of California Press.

Trends in the '90's: NCR/Gallup poll supplement. (1993, October 8). *National Catholic Reporter*.

United States Catholic Conference. (1972). To teach as Jesus did. In *Pastoral letters of the United States Catholic bishops: Volume III* (Publication No. 870). Washington, DC: Author.

United States Catholic Conference. (1976). Teach them. *Origins, 6*, 1-7.

United States Catholic Conference. (1979). *Sharing the light of faith:National catechetical directory for Catholics of the United States*. Washington, DC: Author.

United States Catholic Conference. (1980). *Catholic higher education and the Church's pastoral mission*. Washington, DC: Author.

United States Catholic Conference. (1994a). *Catechism of the Catholic Church.* Vatican City: Libreria Editrice Vaticana.

United States Catholic Conference. (1994b). *A vision statement for catechesis.* Unpublished draft.

United States Catholic Conference. (1992). Nutrition and hydration: Moral and pastoral reflections. *Origins, 21,* 705-712.

United States Catholic Conference. (1990a). Guidelines for doctrinally sound catechetical materials. *Origins, 20,* 429-436.

United States Catholic Conference. (1990b). *A report on the state of catechesis in the United States: Findings and conclusions.* Washington, DC: Author.

Utendorf, J. (1985). Reasons for participation in Roman Catholic lay ministry training programs. *Review of Religious Research, 26,* 281-292.

Verbit, M. (1970). The components and dimensions of religious behavior: Toward a reconceptualization of religiosity. In P. Hammond & B. Johnson (Eds.), *American mosaic: Social patterns of religion in the United States* (pp. 24-39). New York: Random House.

Wach, J. (1944). *Sociology of religion.* Chicago: University of Chicago Press.

Warren, M. (1970). All contributions cheerfully accepted. *Living Light, 7*(4), 20-39.

Weigert, A., & Thomas, D. (1969). Religiosity in 5-D: A critical note. *Social Forces, 48,* 260-263.

About the Author

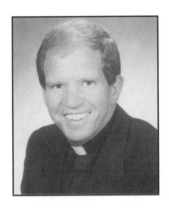

Father Paul W. Galetto, OSA, Ph.D., is an associate professor at Villanova University. This book is a result of his doctoral work in educational administration at The Catholic University of America in Washington, D.C.

Father Galetto completed his studies for priesthood at the Gregorian University in Rome, Italy. He has been a missionary in Nigeria and Peru, where the Augustinians have various apostolic commitments. He has taught high school for ten years at St. Augustine Prep in Richland, N.J., and has been an associate pastor, religious prior, and an elementary school religion teacher in Vineland, N.J. Currently, Father Galetto is the secretary for the board of directors of St. Augustine Prep and a member of the secondary education committee of the Augustinian Province of St. Thomas of Villanova. He regularly gives conferences and workshops in the Greater Philadelphia area.